ChristianNomics

FOR TEENAGERS & YOUNG ADULTS

Joyful Life Publishing

GOD'S MASTER PLAN FOR FINANICIAL FREEDOM

Practical and Spiritual Wisdom For Teenagers & Young Adults to Build a Life of Joy and Prosperity

JERRY LEPRE

Library of Congress Cataloging-in-Publication Data

LePre, Christopher Gerard "Jerry," 1955-
CHRISTIANNOMICS : God's master plan for financial freedom
Practical and spiritual wisdom for teenagers and young adults to build a life of joy and prosperity
Jerry LePre, LLC
p. cm.
Includes bibliographical references

ISBN: **9798337623351**

1. Christian Books & Bibles> Christian Living> Stewardship
2. Teen & Young Adult> Educational> Reference> General
3. Business & Money> Personal Finance> Budget & Money Management.> Budgeting

Printed in the United States of America
Joyful Life Publishing, Destrehan, LA

This book is dedicated to Father Anthony McGinn, S.J. who made a significant impact not only on my life when he was a young Jesuit scholastic but also on the lives of thousands of graduates during his long tenure as president of Jesuit High School New Orleans. Thank you for being part of the Blue Jay mentoring team that made me a man for others – a man of service.

A.M.D.G.
Ad majorem Dei gloriam
For the greater glory of God

IMPORTANT INFORMATION

The intent of this book is to offer information of a general nature. The author does not provide legal, financial, spiritual, investment, or psychological advice. Reading this book does not ensure success of any degree, since success is usually determined, defined, and measured by several factors that vary per individual.

Concepts provided in Chapters 7 and 8 are some of the basic strategies and tactics that helped me stretch and conserve my money. Although successful for me, my tactics may not have the same cost-saving impact or results for you and your family.

Before implementing any tactics, discuss your specific situation with licensed professionals to create financial, investment, and tax saving plans that fit your unique needs, culture, and lifestyle.

Information in this book is subject to change. In the event you use any information in this book, the author, copyright holder, and publisher assume no liability.

Some concepts used in this book are based on information contained in my book "God's Money-Back Guarantee."

By buying and/or reading this book, you agree to hold harmless the author, publisher, and copyright holder for everything resulting from this book.

A special thank you to my former high school classmate John H. Gin, CFP® Private Wealth Advisor and his staff for their help with the investment section of this book.

Table of Contents

CHRISTIANNOMICS

Table of Contents (Continued)

** References found in the Notes section are indicated by a number following a word, sentence, paragraph, or title.*
NOTE: Before implementing any tactic, strategy, or action item found in this book, contact a licensed professional.

Faithkeepers' Prayer

for the Peace and Joy of Prosperity

Dear Lord,

I humbly ask you to bless me with the
wisdom, strength, and patience to fully develop my
time, talents, and treasures as I grow in faith and
maturity as a Christian Adult.
Help me obtain the spiritual and financial peace and
joy promised in your Holy Word.
Teach me how to use your wisdom to form the
foundation of my life with Jesus as its cornerstone.
Upon this divine rock, guide me to build a storehouse
filled with a wealth of blessings so
I may honor you with my loving and unselfish
acts of joyful giving.
Thank you for your unending gifts of
love, grace, and mercy.
Amen.

Realty Struck

Author's Note to Teens & Young Adults

Although it has been a few decades since I started out on my own, I still can relate to the many financial challenges faced today by young adults. The cost of necessities due to inflation has drastically changed since then but the economic challenges facing young people have not.

I remember when I got out of college, I was offered a job as a weekend sports anchor in a small market. I was excited about this opportunity. Then reality struck.

I needed to pay for rent and utilities. I had to buy food and a car which meant a down payment, monthly loan installments, insurance, gasoline, licenses, and upkeep.

I also discovered that you don't get to keep what you earn. The federal, state, and local governments took their share before I got mine.

The fact is: I couldn't afford to take the job. I was forced to accept a lesser local position and live at home with my mom and grandmother. Frustrating. I had to share a 500 square foot NOLA shotgun house with no privacy.

I realized that to escape this financial prison and make it on my own, I had to not only earn more in another field of work but also how to maximize my paycheck.

The wisdom I gained during this time of financial growth came from wise mentors and the countless mistakes I made. Yet this insight laid the foundation for this book whose purpose is to prepare teens and young adults to build a life of financial peace, joy, and prosperity.

Chapter 1

CHRISTIANNOMICS

THE VISION

GETTING STARTED

Victory Verse

"The Lord will guarantee a blessing on everything you do and will fill your storehouses with grain. The Lord your God will bless you in the land He is giving you."

Deuteronomy 28:8 - NLT

GOD'S MASTER PLAN FOR FINANCIAL FREEDOM

The Vision and Mission

"For I can do everything through Christ, who gives me strength." (Philippians 4:13 - NLT)

As a child I knew what it meant to be financially poor. I grew up in a small rundown shotgun double with my mother and grandmother. My father and mother were divorced when I was 2 years old. A few months later, he abandoned me.

My mom worked hard to support us, but career women were paid much less back then. Thus, money was scarce and her routine phrase to me was, "No. We don't have the money for it."

It was years later that I realized how that one statement affected my life. As a young adult, this feeling of "not enough" motivated me to fill the emptiness with the things money could buy.

I put money first. It was all about me and making and spending money. It was not about God.

Although I created and implemented several effective strategies and tactics to create and conserve wealth, money was never enough. I was not happy.

I tried to figure it out but by not putting God first, I lacked the peace and joy of my success. I felt a void; a void that only God could fill.

Fortunately, despite setbacks, numerous mistakes, and several bad choices, God didn't abandon me. With God's grace, I was able to restore and renew my faith.

During my time of growth, I realized God's plan for financial freedom, which is *ChristianNOMICS*™. I learned to combine my practical financial strategies with a solid spiritual foundation and a strong Christian character. Both were strengthened by prayer and Scripture reading.

This powerful combination resulted in the peace and joy of financial freedom. I first shared this insight in my book *God's Money-back Guarantee.*

A lot has happened since I wrote that first book. Back then we connected with people differently. There were no Facebook, YouTube, LinkedIn, and texting.

We used old fashion home phones to talk to a live voice. We sent letters by mail through the post office.

Yet despite these lifestyle changes, the economic challenges we face today are the same.

Fortunately, God's truths and assurances regarding financial freedom remain constant. In fact, achieving God's financial promises of peaceful prosperity are as possible today as they have always been.

Thus, this book teaches God's prayerful promises, principles, and powerful tactics of financial victory for teens and young adults. It offers spiritual and practical wisdom to build a foundation for the future to live a joyful and prosperous life with over 100 ways to keep our hard-earned money.

My practical financial concepts include money saving methods for shopping, reorganizing debt, lowering insurance costs, reducing taxes, lending money by the book (Bible), establishing good credit, and much more.

If you are only interested in living a self-centered and lavish lifestyle, this is not your get-rich-quick book.

Instead, my mission is to engage, empower, and energize teens and young adults to discover the peace and joy of financial freedom. This is the debt-free lifestyle that results from faithfully following *ChristianNOMICS*™, which is God's master plan for financial freedom.

"Instruct those who are rich in this present world not to be conceited or to fix their hope on the uncertainty of riches, but on God, who richly supplies us with all things to enjoy." (1 Timothy 6:17 - NASB)

NOTE: A debt-free lifestyle means we are not a prisoner to unnecessary debt that is caused by bad financial decisions usually resulting from living above our means. When we live debt-free, we are financially free to discover a life of joy, peace, and prosperity. God's path leads to financial freedom. *(Page 90)*

CHRISTIANNOMICS™

Pronounced: (kris'-chən-nom-iks) n.

DEFINITION: The spiritual art and science (non-exact) that studies the economic rules and principles regarding distribution, management, and consumption of wealth, possessions, resources, and assets as they relate to the teachings found in Scripture. It is solely based on the fundamental financial truths, values, and doctrines found in the Bible (Living Word of God).

Simply stated, *ChristianNOMICS*™ is God's master plan to build a debt-free life of joy and prosperity through practical and spiritual wisdom. It includes the prayerful promises, principles, and powerful tactics of financial victory through Christ.

Furthermore, the value of *ChristianNOMICS*™ is much greater than a definition or a theological doctrine. It is living (Chapter 9) a prayer-filled (Chapter 3), disciplined (Chapter 6), and debt-free lifestyle grounded by a strong spiritual foundation (Chapter 4) with the Christian values of Jesus Christ as its cornerstone. Upon this solid rock, our *Christian Financial Character* (Chapter 5) is built with love, integrity, joyful giving, and service.

The divine blueprint for *ChristianNOMICS*™ is provided by God's practical and spiritual wisdom (Chapter 2). This divine design applies proven strategies (Chapter 7) and tactics (Chapter 8) to create, cultivate, celebrate, share, and conserve wealth.

Stewardship: Working for God

"Whatever you do, do your work heartily, as for the Lord rather than for men, knowing that from the Lord you will receive the reward of the inheritance. It is the Lord Christ whom you serve. (Colossians 3:23-24 – NASB)

The best opportunity for a management position with career advancement is found in the Bible. It's called stewardship and we are all qualified.

The definition of a steward is one who is entrusted with the management of property, finances, or other affairs not his own; a keeper.

When applied to Christianity, stewardship shows our commitment to managing the gifts God has entrusted to us. Hence, our success as a steward is measured by our faithfulness instead of accumulated wealth. (Read Luke 16:12 and 1 Timothy 6:20)

In fact, Scripture (Proverbs 15:6 and Psalm 37:16) states a financially free and faithful Christian steward of modest means is richer (rich in spirit) than a selfish millionaire who is leveraged and trapped by financial burden.

According to a gathering of U.S. Catholic Bishops, a Christian steward lives as a disciple of Christ.[1]

The bishops said, "Following Jesus is the work of a lifetime. At every step forward, one is challenged to go further in accepting and loving God's will."

Furthermore, these church leaders deemed faithful stewardship to be a total way of life. This lifestyle is achieved by our personal accountability of our time, talents, and treasures. It's a day-by-day, moment-by-moment commitment, even when life gets tough.

Such a commitment may seem impossible. Yet we are not alone. We have God as our divine architect.

Feel at Home with Your Finances

When it comes to building a peaceful, joyful, and prosperous Christian life (debt-free lifestyle), it's sort of like constructing a home for your finances. So build a house with wisdom, faith, hope, and love. (Read Proverbs 24:3)

God's master plan for financial freedom includes:

- The Blueprint (Chapter 2);
- The Groundwork (Chapter 3);
- The Foundation (Chapter 4);
- The Framework (Chapter 5);
- The Roof (Chapter 6);
- The Walls (Chapter 7); and
- The Interior (Chapter 8).

Chapter 2

God's Financial Wisdom

THE BLUEPRINT

Victory Verses

"With me (God's wisdom) are riches and honor, enduring wealth, and prosperity."

Proverbs 8:18

"Wisdom is a shelter as money is a shelter, but the advantage of knowledge is this: Wisdom preserves those who have it."

Ecclesiastes 7:12

God's Promise of Financial Peace

"Whoever pursues righteousness and love, finds life, prosperity, and honor." (Proverbs 21:21)

As my faith continued to grow and Scripture reading increased, I learned the Bible contains not only spiritual wisdom but also teaches practical advice for handling our finances. Therefore, God wants us to prosper both in spirit and wealth.

In fact, our financial well-being is so important to God that the Bible refers to some aspect or form of wealth in over two thousand verses.[1] These Scriptures empower us to walk in the peace and joy of financial freedom, which is a debt-free lifestyle.

"Blessed are all who fear the Lord, who walk in obedience to Him. You will eat the fruit of your labor; blessings and prosperity will be yours." (Psalm 128:1-2)

To comprehend God's promises for *prosperity*, we must first understand how His meaning of *prosperity* compares to the world's definition.

The world defines prosperity as *the state of financial success, a high level of wealth that is flourishing*. The focus is on money and power.

In contrast, God considers us to be prosperous when we are debt-free to joyfully serve Him and His people with our gifts of time, talents, and treasures. The focus is on God and godly living.

While the world seeks the elusive joy of prosperity, those who follow God know His joy.

"When God gives someone wealth and possessions, and the ability to enjoy them, to accept their lot and be happy in their toil - this is a gift of God." (Ecclesiastes 5:19)

Scripture Reveals God's Blueprint for Financial Independence

The Bible is a timeless source of financial wisdom. It contains God's economic blueprint for building a shelter of wealth.

"All Scripture is inspired by God and is useful to teach us what is true and to make us realize what is wrong in our lives. It corrects us when we are wrong and teaches us to do what is right." (2 Timothy 3:16 - NLT)

God's financial wisdom that is found in or based on Scripture includes: *(All discussed later.)*

- Understanding God's purposes for money;
- Experiencing the meaning of joyful giving;
- Following a Christ-centered financial plan;
- The purpose and need for insurance;
- Paying taxes;
- Investment concepts and strategies;
- Planning for a peaceful retirement;
- Creating a legacy for future generations;
- Living the role of a champion steward; and
- Lending/borrowing money by the book (Bible).

The World's View of Money

Before we continue to discuss God's financial wisdom and His purposes for money, we need to take a look at what the world thinks about money.

Money is defined as any generally accepted medium of exchange that facilitates and simplifies payment for goods and services. The U.S. dollar is a "fiat" currency. Thus, it is not backed by any tangible commodity, but rather it is backed by the *full faith and credit of the United States*. In the past, it was backed by a reserve of equal value of monetary metals.[2]

Paper money becomes legal tender when the issuing government lawfully determines that all creditors must accept this currency in settlement of all debts. It serves as a standard of value for measuring the worth or price of commodities.[3]

However, the real value of any accepted form of money is determined by its purchasing power, which is affected by the conditions and trends of the overall economy.

An economy is the way the production, distribution, trade, and consumption of goods and services determine (1) commodity pricing and supplies, (2) employment and wages, and (3) the purchasing power of money.

The alarming factor about our country's economy is our national debt is growing by an estimated $2 million per minute.[4] The current debt is over $268,000 per taxpayer and is projected to grow by $20 trillion in 2034.[5] [6]

How old will you be in 2034?

God's Primary Purposes for Money

Despite our current fluctuating economic state, God is in charge. Let's do it His way.

If each of us handles our money matters according to God's master plan, the chain reaction will eventually turn financial uncertainty into prosperity.

This economic revival starts by us using our money for God's purposes instead of worshiping money and putting it before God. (Read 1 Timothy 6:10)

Money is a gift from God. It is a tool to serve Him and support His works. Money is not a god.

Money is a gift from God. It is a tool to serve Him and support His works.

"No one can serve two masters. For you will hate one and love the other; you will be devoted to one and despise the other. You cannot serve God and be enslaved to money." (Matthew 6:24 - NLT))

The following are God's four primary purposes for money.

TOOL FOR JOYFUL GIVING (Page 64)

Money is a tool for Christians to joyfully give gifts and offerings to those in need and to perpetuate the growth of God's Church and His Holy Works. Money is not to be worshiped, hoarded, buried, or wasted.

(Read Proverbs 18:16)

STANDARD FOR STEWARDSHIP

Scripture sets the standard for handling our finances as faithful stewards. Are we slothful stewards, mediocre stewards, or champion stewards?

A champion steward is a loyal and faithful Christian of good character who lives a debt-free lifestyle to honor God by serving with his or her time, talents, and treasures. A champion steward exemplifies the truths and values of *ChristianNOMICS*™.

(Read Matthew 25:14-30)

TRANSFER OF CONSIGNMENTS

Since God owns everything in the universe, no one can truly buy or own anything. Thus, when we use the terms *to own, to buy,* or *to purchase,* we mean we are agreeing to act as good stewards when accepting the worldly control and all the responsibilities associated with an item.

This control is consigned to us by another steward in exchange for a payment based on the secular value system of money.

Therefore, God uses money to serve as a secular measurement for transferring worldly responsibilities of stewardship.

(Read Psalm 24:1)

REWARD FOR RIGHTEOUSNESS

God provides money as a blessing to serve as a reward for righteousness. He blesses faithful Christians to empower them to serve and bless others. We are blessed to be a blessing.

(Read 1 Samuel 26:23)

Faith Defeats Obstacles

On our journey to discover the financial rewards, blessings, and opportunities promised by God, we frequently find roadblocks and detours. Despite these challenges, keep the faith by listening to God's wisdom. Become a champion of faith.

In 1 Peter 1:7 (NLT) we learn "These trials will show that your faith is genuine. It is being tested as fire tests and purifies gold - though your faith is far more precious than mere gold. So when your faith remains strong through many trials, it will bring you much praise and glory and honor when Jesus Christ is revealed to the whole world."

Sometimes these challenges are like mountains in our path that either slow us down or stop us.

The only way we conquer our mountain is to climb it step by step.

The only way we conquer our mountain is to climb it step by step. We cannot rush to the top.

Take it slowly, one step, one prayer at a time.

"We can make our plans, but the Lord determines our steps." (Proverbs 16:9 - NLT)

When blessed with God's gifts of perseverance and persistence, there is no mountain or obstacle too high to climb. As Christ instructed, when we have the faith of a champion, we not only conquer our mountain; we can move it.

"Truly I tell you, if you have faith as small as a mustard seed, you can say to this mountain, 'Move from here to there,' and it will move. Nothing will be impossible for you." (Matthew 17:20)

Yet even with this assurance, we become impatient. We want instant results to all of our prayers, especially those for financial help.

Patience is a sign of wisdom, growth, and maturity.

However, patience is a sign of wisdom, growth, and maturity. It allows the time for truth to reveal hidden agendas and lies.

Even though time waits for no one, patiently wait for the right time.

Be patient as stated in Proverbs 13:11, "whoever gathers money little by little makes it grow."

Above all, God wants to help. He hears us as stated in 1 Peter 3:12, "For the eyes of the Lord are on the righteous and His ears are attentive to their prayer."

Yet we wonder; why does He take so long?

Don't worry. God is sovereign. He answers our prayers in His timing. Have faith in knowing that God will respond. God promises His faithful stewards will "spend the rest of their days in prosperity and their years in contentment." (Job 36:11)

Wherever faith is planted, something beautiful will one day bloom if you to take the time and action to make it grow.

Financial Freedom: Faith in Action

"Faith by itself, if it is not accompanied by action, is dead." (James 2:17)

Action brings life to our faith. Since financial freedom plans are alive and growing, we can't become passive or stagnant. Our financial victory is won by applying God's wisdom to our actions and adapting our actions to current conditions without losing the spirit of God's message.

Taking action in this manner isn't easy. It takes work, since God wants us to become financially free not freeloaders. When we do our best; God will do the rest. God actively works with us, through us, and through others. (Read Proverbs 14:23 and 15:22)

To put faith into action we need to be prayerfully prepared (Chapter 3) to build our solid spiritual foundation (Chapter 4) and strong Christian Character (Chapter 5). We are then ready to implement practical proven strategies (Chapter 7) and tactics (Chapter 8) to live a debt-free lifestyle.

Since the journey to success is seldom walked alone, the Lord provides support from our family, church, friends, mentors, and professional advisors.

Pray that God sends us the right people, at the right time, for the right reasons. Pray that our support group fully understands God's message, wisdom, and how to apply its meaning to the Lord's plan for us. (Read Proverbs 14:15)

Faith in action sows the seeds of victory.

God is the Best Bet

In today's "microwave" instant society that is influenced by social media and peer pressure, it's hard for many teens and young adults to tackle challenges without being persuaded or manipulated by a third party who often has a hidden agenda. This is especially true when young people act too quickly without thinking.

These impulsive decision makers react to situations instead of responding with prayer, wise Christian counseling, and proactive planning. Many of these young people who lack good judgement take part in get-rich-quick schemes that fail, succumb to drug and alcohol abuse, or participate in immoral or illegal activities while others are addicted to compulsive buying or obsessively gambling away their money at casinos or on lottery tickets.

All of these compulsive worldly activities eventually lead to financial ruin since these people are gambling with their future.

These gamblers put their trust, their faith, and their expectations of happiness on the wrong things instead of God. Yet God is the only sure bet for peaceful prosperity.

The wealth and prosperity that God promises is not based on chance. It is not based on luck.

It is based on our faith and obedience to actively follow His wisdom and His instructions.

There are several authors, television evangelists, and speakers who can motivate you if that is all you want.

But when it comes to financial independence, Christians need more than a self-centered pep talk filled with comforting lies that give false hope. Instead faithful Christians seek God as the strength and source of their financial peace and joy.

Always remember, wherever faith leads us, the Lord will be there. God's Word puts the odds in our favor.

"Your word is a lamp to guide my feet and a light for my path." (Psalm 119:105 - NLT)

God is the best bet. You can bet on it.

Chapter 3
Prayerful Preparation
THE GROUNDWORK

Victory Verse

"And pray in the Spirit on all occasions with all kinds of prayers and requests. With this in mind, be alert and always keep on praying for all the Lord's people."

Ephesians 6:18

The Power of Prayer

"Therefore I tell you, whatever you ask for in prayer, believe that you have received it, and it will be yours." (Mark 11:24)

Prayer is the groundwork for miracles, since miracles originate from prayer. I consider prayer time valuable. To me prayer is a God-given gift allowing all of us to establish a divine connection of communication with our Lord.

My private prayer time isn't confined to early in the morning or late at night. I pray during the day. In fact, I often pray while driving in my car, which may explain why I have avoided many near accidents.

The important thing is prayers are answered. Maybe not immediately but when we are faithful, God will provide the answers we seek.

Prayer empowers us to understand God's purpose for us through His wisdom, grace, and mercy. God's sovereignty as our intercessor is shown by answered prayers.

Unfortunately, many Christians don't properly use this gift of communicating with God. These Christians forget the power of prayer is found in the dialogue. They forget to listen for the answers they seek.

"Ask and it will be given to you; seek and you will find; knock and the door will be opened to you. For everyone who asks receives; the one who seeks finds; and to the one who knocks, the door will be opened." (Luke 11:9-10)

Jesus teaches in Luke that when we make prayer an essential part of our lives, our invocations to God are answered. This includes financial requests.

Thus, before building a joyful life of financial freedom, we must build a solid prayer life. Prayer changes a slothful steward into a champion steward.

Prayer changes a slothful steward into a champion steward.

Therefore, when we face the adversities of life, prayer must be our first response and not done as our last resort.

Furthermore, prayer is a time for self-evaluation. This prayerful assessment, when guided by the Holy Spirit, awakens and humbles us to be accountable for our past mistakes.

Accountability means accepting responsibility for our actions while facing its consequences. By facing these facts, we identify the sources and reasons (not excuses) for our past financial shortcomings. As a result, we are better equipped to avoid them in the future.

Keys for Prayerful Preparation

"This is the confidence we have in approaching God: that if we ask anything according to His will, He hears us. And if we know that He hears us - whatever we ask - we know that we have what we asked of Him." (1 John 5:14-15)

To understand the wisdom, power, and inspiration of God's Word, it's important to get back to the basic of prayer by applying *Nine Spiritual Acts of Prayerful Preparation*.

1: Believe that God is the all-powerful creator.

"You are the God who performs miracles; you display your power among the peoples." (Psalm 77:14)

The debt-filled lifestyle caused by our human nature is impossible to conquer without the power of God. As we prayerfully prepare for our financial miracle, we discover that it's only through God's almighty power we are able to change, grow, and learn.

2: Humble ourselves to God.

"Humble yourself before the Lord, and He will lift you up." (James 4:10)

It takes humility to honestly admit to our financial mistakes, shortcomings, and character flaws. By humbly and prayerfully surrendering to God's will, we are freed from the emotional burden of debt.

3: Admit we are powerless without God.

"He gives strength to the weary and increases the power of the weak." (Isaiah 40:29)

By realizing we are weak without divine intervention, we allow grace to enlighten and heal our mind, body, and soul. It is through God's power (not our power) that we are empowered to achieve financial freedom.

(Read Philippians 4:13 - NLT)

4: Confess our weaknesses to God and friends.

"Therefore confess your sins to each other and pray for each other so that you may be healed. The prayer of a righteous person is powerful and effective." (James 5:16)

Before we can end our sinful ways, freely admit to our Heavenly Father and to our trusted friends that we are responsible for our actions.

It was our choice to turn away from God, just as it is our choice now to return to His loving protection. Through our prayer of confession, God releases us from the chains of financial burdens.

5: Give praises of thanksgiving to God.

"I will be glad and rejoice in you; I will sing the praises of your name, O Most High." (Psalm 9:2)

"Do not be anxious about anything, but in every situation, by prayer and petition, with thanksgiving, present your requests to God." (Philippians 4:6)

> It is through His (God's) love, mercy, and saving grace that we are renewed and our prayer requests are answered.

When we praise God, our provider and financial healer, we profess our thanks to Him for all He has given us in the past and for all that will be granted to us in the future. Praise, when offered from a repentant heart, serves as our request for God's redeeming power. It is through His love, mercy, and saving grace that we are renewed and our prayer requests are answered.

6: Turn our decisions over to God.

"But seek first His kingdom and His righteousness, and all these things will be given to you as well. Therefore do not worry about tomorrow, for tomorrow will worry about itself." (Matthew 6:33-34)

In life, we often face difficult choices that will affect us and our families for the rest of our lives. Our decision making, which is often pressured by worldly influences, can be overwhelming, especially when it comes to our finances.

Yet God has His solutions for all of our problems. All we need to do is turn to our Lord for His wisdom and guidance. Our financial solutions are found when we prayerfully seek His answers and surrender to His direction.

"Cast your cares on the Lord and He will sustain you; He will never let the righteous be shaken." (Psalm 55:22)

7: Pray for forgiveness and healing.

"If my people, who are called by my name, will humble themselves and pray and seek my face and turn from their wicked ways, then will I hear from heaven and I will forgive their sin and will heal their land." (2 Chronicles 7:14)

Our God is a forgiving God who desires to heal us in every way. God is *Jehovah Rapha,* meaning "the God who heals." He is the cure for painful finances.

8: Be specific with prayer requests.

When asking God for our prayerful requests, be specific. By doing this, we have no doubt for what we seek. Our petitions are accurately recorded in both heaven and earth with no misunderstanding. Thus, we can specifically note each miracle as it comes to us so we can give thanks and praise to God.

9: Pray from the heart.

Prayer is more than just words. God didn't intend it to be an intellectual exercise between Him and us. The purest form of prayer is our simple and sincere expression of faith regarding what our heart desires. Pray from the heart and not from the head. In this way, as our prayers go up, God's provisions come down.

Chapter 4

Spiritual Foundation

THE FOUNDATION WITH JESUS AS OUR CORNERSTONE

Victory Verse

"As you come to Him, the living Stone - rejected by humans but chosen by God and precious to Him - you also, like living stones, are being built into a spiritual house…."

1 Peter 2:4-5

A Christian Financial Foundation

"Suppose one of you wants to build a tower. Won't you first sit down and estimate the cost to see if you have enough money to complete it? For if you lay the foundation and are unable to finish it, everyone who sees it will ridicule you." (Luke 14:28-29)

As a child, I was blessed to have had a great Sunday school teacher who instilled in me an intense passion for Scripture and Bible stories. Her guidance, combined with daily prayer and Scripture reading, enabled me to start building a Christian foundation at an early age.

I am grateful for this solid groundwork of spiritual truths and fundamental virtues. In fact, it proved to be my saving grace of hope.

As I stated earlier, I once strayed from my Christian core and became worldly and materialistic. I bought expensive cars, jewelry, and suits. I had to have it all, but all was never enough. I was trying to fill a void.

Had I continued on that path I would now be in financial ruin. But with God's grace, along with the Christian base of my childhood, I was able to change my path to one that guided me to peace and joy. My reboot started by placing the Christian values of Jesus as the cornerstone of my life and finances.

A cornerstone (or setting stone) is the first stone placed in a foundation. All the other stones are set in alignment to this stone. A cornerstone determines the position of the whole structure.

Forming the Spiritual Foundation

"But God's truth stands firm like a foundation of stone with this inscription: The Lord knows those who are His and all who belong to the Lord must turn away from evil." (2 Timothy 2:19 - NLT)

With Christ as our cornerstone, we each form our foundation for spiritual growth and maturity with five fundamental essentials. A solid spiritual base enables us to stand firm and strong against the deceptive elements of the world.

"Righteousness and justice are the foundation of your throne. Unfailing love and truth walk before you as attendants." (Psalm 89:14 - NLT)

Essentials for Forming a Spiritual Foundation

- Be still and seek God.
  (Read Psalm 46:10 and Isaiah 55:6)
- Connect with God and His Church.
  (Read Ephesians 4:16 and Matthew 18:20)
- Discover and reflect on God's Words of wisdom.
  (Chapter 2)
- Live a rock-solid prayer life.
  (Chapter 3)
- Love abundantly and unconditionally.
  (Read 1 Corinthians 13:4-8 and Mark 12:30-31)

Our spiritual foundations are supported by spiritual truths and strengthened with virtues.

Spiritual Truths Provide Support

In southern Louisiana, most of our land is sinking. As a result, we use pilings to support the foundations for our homes and buildings. Pilings keep our structures level and prevent them from sinking.

Spiritual truths are like that too. These five timeless truths keep our spiritual foundation level and prevent us from sinking into a life that offends God and leads to financial ruin.

1: God loves us.

"For God so loved the world that He gave His one and only Son…." (John 3:16)

God created the riches of the universe as a sign of His love for us. He uses them to bless us through spiritual, emotional, and financial gifts.

2: God is for us.

"If God is for us, who can be against us?" (Romans 8:31)

God doesn't want us to fail. When we surrender to His will, we are victorious. Even in our darkest hours, we are not alone. God is with us to comfort, help, and strengthen us. (Read Psalm 23:4)

"Don't be afraid, for I am with you. Don't be discouraged, for I am your God. I will strengthen you and help you with my victorious right hand." (Isaiah 41:10 - NLT)

3: God has a glorious plan of prosperity for us.

"If they listen and obey God, they will be blessed with prosperity throughout their lives. All their years will be pleasant." (Job 36:11 - NLT)

God desires His faithful people to discover and follow His plan of financial wisdom. When we do, He blesses us with a life of peaceful and joyful prosperity.

4: God redeems and renews us through Christ.

"Praise be to the Lord, the God of Israel, because He has come to His people and redeemed them." (Luke 1:68)

When we place Christian values as the cornerstone of our finances, new life is given to our economic dealings. This fresh start requires us to handle all of our financial matters in a *Christ-like* manner. This includes how we interact with Christians and non-Christians in money transactions.

5: God sends us His Holy Spirit for enlightenment.

"But the Advocate, the Holy Spirit, whom the Father will send in my name, will teach you all things and will remind you of everything I have said to you." (John 14:26)

Since the worldly forces that cause financial abuse continue to attack, we need the Holy Spirit to guide us away from temptations. When we walk away from the Spirit, we walk toward economic decay. When we walk with the Spirit, we walk toward the peace and joy of financial freedom.

Virtues Strengthen our Foundation to Prevent Cracking

"Fix your thoughts on what is true, and honorable, and right, and pure, and lovely, and admirable. Think about things that are excellent and worthy of praise." (Philippians 4:8 - NLT)

As the foundations of our structures age and face the stress of outside conditions, some will crack. It may start off small, but the cracks will grow. If these fractures aren't repaired, the whole structure will eventually suffer serious damage.

In regard to our spiritual foundation, virtues provide the inner strength to keep us from cracking under the stress and pressures of daily life.

A virtue is a fundamental quality, trait, practice, or attitude of moral righteousness. It develops our ethics and values that shape our core as champion stewards.

Therefore, before building upon our solid foundation for both spiritual and financial prosperity, the *Virtues* of faith, hope, and charity (known as the *Theological Virtues*) along with fortitude, justice, prudence, and temperance (known as the *Cardinal Virtues*) must be firmly in place.

The *Theological Virtues* originate directly from God's grace while the *Cardinal Virtues* originate from human effort cultivated through God's grace.

Theological Virtues

FAITH is "the confidence in what we hope for and assurance about what we do not see."(Hebrews 11.1)

Faith, the first of the *Theological Virtues,* is our belief in the existence of the unseen Holy Trinity. Without faith, we cannot love, obey, or worship God.

When we have faith in our finances, we believe in God's promises of prosperity. Faith has no boundaries; it has no limitations except those that we create.

HOPE is an expectation, longing, and desire for a certain thing to happen. It is through our hope for eternal life that we, as Christians, understand God's master plan of salvation.

In regard to our treasures, hope encourages us to seek our promised expectations of prosperity despite worldly setbacks.

"You are my refuge and my shield; I have put my hope in your word." (Psalm 119:114)

CHARITY is the gift of time, talents, and treasures to those in need of help. These unselfish acts of joyful giving are compassionate responses to the love and charity that God has shown to us. Acts of charity define our foundation for joyful giving.

"One person gives freely, yet gains even more; another withholds unduly, but comes to poverty." (Proverbs 11:24)

Cardinal Virtues

FORTITUDE is the state of mind that energizes and empowers believers to stand strong with courage against all the adversities, suffering, and tragedies that occur in our lives. This virtue defends us from giving up and giving in to temptations. It prevents us from having the victim mentality.

"Be on guard; stand firm in the faith; be courageous; be strong." (1 Corinthians 16:13)

JUSTICE is the ability to judge fairly and impartially by rendering with mercy and righteousness what is due or merited in order to conform to decrees.

"Do not pervert justice or show partiality. Do not accept a bribe, for a bribe blinds the eyes of the wise and twists the words of the innocent. Follow justice and justice alone, so that you may live and possess the land the Lord your God is giving you." (Deuteronomy 16:19-20)

PRUDENCE is the discernment through wisdom and knowledge by which Christian stewards decide between what is morally right and what is morally wrong. It empowers believers to choose to do good works and avoid evil ways.

"I, wisdom, dwell together with prudence; I possess knowledge and discretion." (Proverbs 8:12)

TEMPERANCE is the self-restraint, discipline, and accountability by which we control worldly passions, desires, and emotions through moderation. Temperance prevents greed and indulgence.

"Teach the older men to be temperate, worthy of respect, self-controlled, and sound in faith, in love, and in endurance." (Titus 2:2)

With virtues in place, we are ready to build our Christian Financial Character (Chapter 5).

"By the grace God has given me, I laid a foundation as a wise builder, and someone else is building on it. But each one should build with care. For no one can lay any foundation other than the one already laid, which is Jesus Christ." (1 Corinthians 3: 10-11)

Do What Jesus Would Do™

Several years ago, it was popular for Christians to wear wrist bands with the caption "WWJD" that stood for "What would Jesus do?"

Although it prompted us to consider doing the right thing, it didn't compel us to do the right thing.

Therefore, when we place Jesus as the cornerstone of our foundation, we DWJWD™ - *Do what Jesus would do!* (Read James 1:22 - NLT)

Chapter 5

C.H.R.I.S.T. Concepts

THE FRAMEWORK OF OUR CHRISTIAN FINANCIAL CHARACTER

Victory Verses

"I came that they may have life, and have it abundantly."

John 10:10 NASB

"Jesus answered, *I am the way, and the truth, and the life. No one comes to the Father except through me."*

John 14:6

Building with the Framework of the C.H.R.I.S.T. Concepts

"They are like a man building a house, who dug down deep and laid the foundation on rock. When a flood came, the torrent struck that house but could not shake it, because it was well built." (Luke 6:48)

Champion stewards survive the challenges of life because their *Christian Financial Character* is well built on a solid foundation with Christ as its cornerstone. (Read Psalm 46:1)

As I started to rebuild my life, like every good builder, I needed good tools. With direction from God's financial blueprint and support from *Spiritual Truths* and *Virtues* (discussed earlier), I discovered six character building tools to frame my *Christian Financial Character.*

An easy way to remember these framing tools, which I call the *C.H.R.I.S.T Concepts,* is to let each one be represented by a letter in the name of CHRIST.

C ommitment

H abit Modification

R esist Temptations

I ntegrity Ethics

S ervice *(Serve with the Heart of a Servant)*

T ithing *(Transform Tithing into Joyful Giving)*

"C" Commitment

"And may your hearts be fully committed to the Lord our God, to live by His decrees and obey His commands." (1 Kings 8:61)

A commitment to excellence is a slogan used by many companies. Yet it is seldom used by Christians to describe their commitment to stewardship.

Therefore, the first letter "C" of our *CHRIST Concepts* is for *commitment*. A total lasting commitment, not just a partial or short-lived pledge, is essential for Christians to become financial winners in this materialistic world.

However, a total commitment is rarely given by anyone today. Almost everyone seems content to do just enough to get by.

Pride in a job well done is almost impossible to find. We accept poor to average performance as a way of life. The word quality is often forgotten for the sake of quantity. What we see is a total lack of commitment towards work ethics and behavior.

This type of performance is not acceptable if we want Christ to be the center of our lives and financial needs. The key to success is a total commitment to our Lord.

Once we let Him into our hearts, we will never face another problem or crisis alone.

"Commit your actions to the Lord, and your plans will succeed." (Proverbs 16:3 - NLT)

"H" Habit Modification

"Don't copy the behavior and customs of this world, but let God transform you into a new person by changing the way you think. Then you will learn to know God's will for you, which is good and pleasing and perfect." (Romans 12:2 - NLT)

A habit is defined as an instinct, practice, or action that is an automatic or a spontaneous response or reaction to a specific situation. It is based on programmed conditioning or experiences.

Breaking a habit can happen immediately or it can take time for a new habit to form. Depending on the expert, it takes from 21 to 66 or as many as 90 consecutive days of behavior change to form a habit.[1]

Yet if you put your hand on a hot stove, you immediately know not to do that again. In this case, change is spontaneous. You don't even need 21 days to learn to avoid the hot stove.

Therefore, we break the cycle of bad habits with *habit modification*, the "H" of our *CHRIST Concepts*.

Our financial freedom is achieved by breaking our bad, losing financial habits and replacing them with God's winning ways.

This transformation occurs through the conviction of our faith, which is strengthened by daily devotion, daily prayer, and daily tactics that fit a moderate and reasonable lifestyle.

"R" Resist Temptation

"And lead us not into temptation." (Luke 11:4)

Every day we are constantly attacked by the forces of temptation. No matter where we go, some form of enticement is trying to persuade or manipulate us to make bad financial decisions. These poor choices take away our peace and joy.

Sources of temptation feed on the selfishness and greediness of human nature. Succumbing to temptation results in overspending, financial ruin, and often bankruptcy.

Though these enticements are often disguised or subliminal, the gift of discernment from the Holy Spirit unmasks these hidden temptations.

Resisting temptation, the "R" of our *C.H.R.I.S.T. Concepts,* is the most challenging concept for me to follow. At times, I struggle to resist my materialistic desires that were once the focus of my life.

But I don't face temptation alone. God is with me. With God, we stand strong. Without God, escaping the forces of temptation would be almost impossible.

Be assured, we will not be tempted beyond our strength.

"No temptation has overtaken you except what is common to mankind. And God is faithful; He will not let you be tempted beyond what you can bear. But when you are tempted, He will also provide a way out so that you can endure it." (1 Corinthians 10:13)

"Therefore put on the full armor of God, so that when the day of evil comes, you may be able to stand your ground, and after you have done everything, to stand. Stand firm then, with the belt of truth buckled around your waist, with the breastplate of righteousness in place, and with your feet fitted with the readiness that comes from the gospel of peace. In addition to all this, take up the shield of faith, with which you can extinguish all the flaming arrows of the evil one. Take the helmet of salvation and the sword of the Spirit, which is the word of God." (Ephesians 6:13-17)

With the full protection of God, we conquer impulsive buying...

With the protection of God, we boldly conquer impulsive buying, resist temptations, and guard our finances from sales pressure and enticements. Our spiritual armor is strengthened when we follow these six steps to defeat the power of financial enticements.

Six Steps to Conquer Temptation

1: Identify our vulnerabilities.

Admitting to our weaknesses, which guided us to financial failure, is the first step, according to Dr. Rhonda Kelley (Author of *Divine Discipline)*. Once we understand our short comings, we can work at confronting these problems, which enable us to develop solutions.

2: Avoid contact with sources of sin.

The roots of temptation are everywhere. So stay away from the people, places, and things that entice us. Kelley states alluring situations can be averted if we take control of our lifestyle.

3: Pray for divine help in unavoidable situations.

Pray for spiritual guidance when we are unable to avoid temptations. The armor that protects us during our daily challenges is fortified when we call to the Lord, who is the rock of our foundation.

4: Pray for strength during times of weakness.

The most common response to adversities, rejections, and disappointments is to seek pleasure through overindulgence. To some this means overeating or excessive drinking, while others have a compulsion to buy expensive luxuries.

During these tough times, though God may appear to be silent to our pleas, He isn't. He is fulfilling His plan for us in accordance with His divine timetable. Never let these discouragements make us easy prey for Satan.

Don't allow misfortune to weaken our faith! Bad behavior will not eliminate our troubles nor will it solve our problems. Solutions are not found in extravagance. The greatest supporter needed to guide us during our trials is God.

5: Don't justify occasional financial failings.

We can't be a part-time Christian only when we feel like it. If we truly desire the financial freedom that results from a Christ-centered lifestyle, we must not take an intermittent detour from our path to our promised prosperity. Occasional wrongful behavior is not a reward for many good actions.

6: Recognize enticements.

Don't be fooled by their deceptive masquerade. To conquer the allurement of temptation, it is necessary to recognize the following seven enticements that attack us daily.

GREED is the never-ending, insensitive, never satisfied, and self-centered act of extreme longing for excessive possessions, especially wealth.

"Beware. Guard against every kind of greed. Life is not measured by how much you own." (Luke 12:15 NLT)

POWER is the forceful ability to control people and take possessions.

"Not by might nor by power, but by my Spirit, says the Lord Almighty." (Zechariah 4:6)

SELFISHNESS is caring only for your own interests and comforts.

"Do nothing out of selfish ambition or vain conceit. Rather, in humility value others above yourselves." (Philippians 2:3)

EGOCENTRIC PLEASURE is self-centered satisfaction and enjoyment without regards to others.

"People will be lovers of themselves, lovers of money, boastful, proud, abusive, disobedient to their parents, ungrateful, unholy, without love, unforgiving, slanderous, without self-control, brutal, not lovers of good, treacherous, rash, conceited, lovers of pleasure rather than lovers of God." (2 Timothy 3:2-4)

JEALOUSY is the act of coveting the possessions or status of others.

"And you still aren't ready, for you are still controlled by your sinful nature. You are jealous of one another and quarrel with each other. Doesn't that prove you are controlled by your sinful nature? Aren't you living like people of the world?" (1 Corinthians 3:2-3–NLT)

GLUTTONY is the indulgent and excessive submission to satisfy earthly gratification.

"Do not join those who drink too much wine or gorge themselves on meat, for drunkards and gluttons become poor, and drowsiness clothes them in rags." (Proverbs 23:20-21)

LUST is overwhelming desire. It's the endless appetite, passion, or obsession for possessions or people.

"For everything in the world - the lust of the flesh, the lust of the eyes, and the pride of life - comes not from the Father but from the world." (1 John 2:16)

"I" Integrity Ethics

"People with integrity walk safely, but those who follow crooked paths will be exposed." (Proverbs 10:9 - NLT)

Integrity begins internally for it comes from the core of our character. Integrity is our decision to do the right thing, even if it's not the best thing for us.

As Christians, we exemplify God's Word. This is especially true when dealing with our finances.

"In everything set an example by doing what is good. In your teaching show integrity, seriousness, and soundness of speech that cannot be condemned, so that those who oppose you may be ashamed because they have nothing bad to say about us." (Titus 2:7-8)

In Chapter 4, we built our solid foundation. Now, we are equipped to enhance the framework of our *Christian Financial Character* with integrity, which represents the "I" of our *CHRIST Concepts.*

...more concerned about being politically correct instead of being Biblically correct.

Sadly, too many people have forsaken the meaning of integrity. They have strayed from God's path to a path of perversion filled with lies and deceit.

These people are unprepared to do the right thing. They are more concerned about being *politically correct* instead of being *Biblically correct.*

Instead of turning within to develop character as taught by God's Word, many prefer to *turn on* to themselves. These people are obsessed with associating acceptance, fortune, fame, and success with their often phony outward facade instead of cultivating a good character.

The solid moral beliefs in quality work that built our civilization have too often been forgotten and replaced with laziness, lies, and cover-ups.

"Above all else, guard your heart, for everything you do flows from it. Keep your mouth free of perversity; keep corrupt talk far from your lips." (Proverbs 4:23-24)

Furthermore, the practice of putting a *spin* on the truth (lying) is considered more and more an acceptable practice. This popularity for *spinning* is due to our unwillingness to accept accountability.

This wrong philosophy professes free interpretation and justification of laws, principles, and rules based on current desires without regard to the spirit and fundamental truth of the law as established by God.

In contrast, God's Word adapts the fundamental truth and spirit of the law to apply to current events without compromising the integrity of moral principles, virtues, and values.

As society comes to a crossroad, it is evident that we, individually and collectively, need to return to a high ethical standard of integrity. This was the standard that made our civilization great. Our future depends on it.

"S" Service (Heart of a Servant)

"Everybody can be great...because anybody can serve. You don't have to have a college degree to serve. You don't have to make your subject and verb agree to serve. You only need a heart full of grace. A soul generated by love," Dr. Martin Luther King, Jr. said.

Servants come in many varieties. They include waitpersons at restaurants, orderlies in hospitals, and first responders who save lives, as well as great business, civic, and political leaders. No matter the title, great servants are dedicated to serve.

Although the word *service* has many meanings, our focus is on the definition of "assistance or benefit afforded another."

The book of Matthew states "to be great, a person must have the heart of a servant." To a champion steward, service is a vocation and not a job. It's a gift freely given and not forced out of duty. Our primary purpose as a Christian is rooted in service, since Christ was an example of a servant leader.

"Whoever wants to become great among you must be your servant." (Matthew 20:26)

A person with the servant's H.E.A.R.T. is *humble, enthusiastic, attentive, respectful,* and *trustworthy.*

According to religious leaders, those who act with the heart of a servant are almost always blessed more than the ones who are served.

Humble - Humility is a virtue common to great servers who keep a low profile and do not promote themselves. This is especially true for first responders who serve with compassion, humility, and honor.

"He guides the humble in what is right and teaches them His way." (Psalm 25:9)

According to author and Pastor Chan Nam Chen, servants "put on the apron of humility." Chen believes that even when honored, servants are free of pride, vanity, arrogance, and personal agendas while keeping a low but confident profile.

Enthusiastic - Great servants are enthusiastic about serving. The positive energy generated by enthusiasm is crucial to making the service process a great experience. Excitement is contagious and can transform someone being served with a negative mindset into one with a positive outlook.

"Never be lacking in zeal, but keep your spiritual fervor, serving the Lord." (Romans 12:11)

Attentive - Great servers are attentive to the legitimate requests, needs, and desires of those they serve. It is an unselfish commitment to do, within reason, whatever it takes to make sure the person or persons being served feel special. Attentive servers are proactive. They anticipate what services are required.

Respectful - One of the primary roles of people who serve is to be respectful to the one or more people they are serving. Respect allows the server to treat others with dignity, appreciation, and consideration.

"Stand up in the presence of the aged, show respect for the elderly and revere your God." (Leviticus 19:32)

However, sometimes a person doesn't earn respect or isn't liked. If you can't respect or like the person you are serving, honor his or her position.

"So in everything, do to others what you would have them do to you." (Matthew 7:12)

Trustworthy - Obedience, dependability, responsibility, loyalty, and honesty are the key qualities that make a server trustworthy. Without trust, a servant's heart will not be complete even when the first four traits (humility, enthusiasm, attentiveness, and respectfulness) are there.

When servers are trustworthy, they are relied upon. When they make commitments, others know they will do all that it takes to honor their promises and fulfill expectations.

However, according to Wisdom Commons, this does not mean that a trustworthy person will never let others down. "Rather, it is an attitude and a pattern of behavior that honors the trust…."

"Well done, my good servant! His master replied. Because you have been trustworthy in a very small matter, take charge of ten cities." (Luke 19:17)

Trustworthiness reaches its pinnacle when our words and actions reflect our inner thoughts, objectives, and intentions. This high level of being trustworthy is the heartbeat of great service. (Read Proverbs 12:22)

When it comes to having the H.E.A.R.T. of a servant, do you need a transplant?

"I will give you a new heart and put a new spirit in you; I will remove from you your heart of stone...." (Ezekiel 36:26)

"T" Tithing (Joyful Giving)

Although tithing is not part of the Catholic faith, it is important to understand the concept.

The word tithe is derived from a Greek word translated as a tenth of a whole. According to Jewish law, there were three tithes that commanded the Jewish people to give 10% (per tithe) of their prosperity to specific purposes.[2]

Each tithe had its own time period, legal restrictions, gifting schedule, and distribution process. The tithe observed today by many Christian faiths is based on the Levitical or sacred tithe that was designated for Levite priests and for the upkeep of the temple (God's Church).[3]

Though Christ does not specifically demand tithing, He taught that He came to fulfill Old Testament laws.

Thus, Jesus, by His Grace, transformed this Old Testament Law into a fundamental act of joyful giving. This is an act of our love, sacrifice, praise, and gratitude to God and His Church.

"You must each decide in your heart how much to give. And don't give reluctantly or in response to pressure. For God loves a person who gives cheerfully." (2 Corinthians 9:7 - NLT)

Joyful giving, unlike a tithe, has no limits and no boundaries. It is not given out of duty, guilt, or obligation. It is freely given with unselfish (Agape) love and without motives and agendas.

Joyful giving creates a rich abundance of peace and joy for both the giver and receiver. This act is the abundance factor of *ChristianNOMICS*™.

Seven Truths of Joyful Giving[4]

"For it is in giving that we receive," St. Francis of Assisi said in the *Prayer of St. Francis*.

1. You can't value a gift by its price tag.

In the parable of the Widow's Offering (Mark 12:41-44), Jesus taught that the value of gifts should not only be treasured by their cost. Additionally, many Scripture verses state gifts can be intangible, such as giving our time, talents, hugs, smiles, joy, laughter, and the most valuable gift of unselfish love.

2. You can't give what you don't have.

Although it is obvious that you can't give away what you don't possess, once we take a deeper look into the meaning of this statement, we discover its fundamental value. From the superficial perspective, it is easy to understand if you don't have money, you can't give much in the way of monetary gifts.

However, once we get past the superficial concept of giving, we look inward to discover what is in our core character. We then ask this personal question, "What do I have inside of me to give?"

Is it a wealth of joy, love, laughter, and kindness or are you filled with an abundance of anger, hatred, bigotry, and pain? Whatever fills your core is what you have to give. You can't give love when you don't have love to give, and you can't give joy when all you have inside of you is anger. (Read Luke 6:45)

In spite of this, if all you have to give comes from a sour core, you can water it down with positive thoughts and sweeten it with loving and kind words. Then, you will take something sour and turn it into something refreshing just like you do when you make lemonade.

3. You can't give what you don't know you have.

We are all valuable to God who has blessed us with special and unique spiritual gifts and worldly talents and skills. Some of these blessings are obvious, but some may be hidden. (Read Romans 12:6)

God blessed us so we can bless others. Pray that you discover and nurture these hidden abilities to share with others in a positive way. Be blessed to be a blessing.

4. You can't receive if your storehouse is full.

The blessings given to us by God are not meant to be hoarded. God's spiritual, physical, emotional, and mental blessings were given to each of us to be shared just as we are commanded to share the message of His Son Jesus Christ, who is God's greatest gift.

If we hoard our gifts, there isn't room for us to receive any new gifts. In the same way, if we keep our love from reaching out, we don't have room in our hearts to be loved. By giving away what we have, we open a space to attract fresh gifts to take its place. (Read Proverbs 11:25)

5. You can't fully appreciate a gift without a thank you.

According to evangelist Billy Graham, "An ungrateful heart is a heart that is cold toward God and indifferent to His mercy and love."

In the same way, when we don't say thank you to anyone giving us a gift, no matter how big or small, we are acting cold, indifferent, and lack respect toward that person. Thus, the uncaring receiver doesn't experience the full joy of the act of giving. (Read Thessalonians 5:16-18)

The acknowledgement of a "thank you" is just as important to the receiver of a gift as it is to the giver. Although the giver may have hurt feelings due to a lack of appreciation, the receiver will not experience the joy of the gift when a thankful response is not offered.

Sincere appreciation completes the connection of the giving cycle.

6. **You can't get sick of giving.**

According to scientists, people who receive an act of kindness have their serotonin (blood protein) levels raised and their immune system enhanced as a result of the gift. This health benefit is also true for the giver and those who observe the joyful act of giving.[2]

7. **You can't outgive giving.** *(You can't outgive God.)*

Although the Apostle Paul writes in the ninth chapter of his second letter to the Corinthians about the blessings gained from being generous, the apostle is not giving us the blueprint for a get-rich-quick scheme. The key concept throughout this Scripture is "having enough of everything." It's not to get rich financially.

If we only give to get, we miss God's blessing.

However, when we give with a joyful spirit, we can't outgive God. In other words, when we give unselfishly, generously, and not expecting anything in return, we will receive more than we ever wanted.

As a result, we have more of our time, talents, treasures, love, joy, and wisdom to joyfully give. The cycle of giving will continue and multiply.

Chapter 6

Divine Discipline

THE ROOF OF PROTECTION
(GOD'S COVERING OF GRACE)

Victory Verse

"For lack of discipline they will die,
led astray by their own great folly."

Proverbs 5:23

Divine Discipline Originates from God's Protection of Grace

"God's way is perfect. All the Lord's promises prove true. He is the shield for all who look to Him for protection." (Psalm 18:30 - NLT)

Once our financial character is prudently framed, we need God's covering of protection (roof) that comes from His divine grace.

"For sin shall no longer be your master, because you are not under the law, but under grace." (Romans 6:14)

Divine grace is God choosing to cover us with His blessings of favor, kindness, protection, and peace. It is through His grace that we mature as stewards through divine discipline.

As I said earlier, if I had continued to make foolish decisions, I would now be financially ruined. I thank God that by His love and grace I was empowered with the discipline and courage to change.

"He who disregards discipline comes to poverty and shame, but whoever heeds correction is honored." (Proverbs 13:18)

However, some respected Christian financial teachers don't always apply God's love and grace to discipline. They believe the best way for most people to achieve financial freedom is by making extreme sacrifices.

I do not agree. Although, tough love may be needed in rare cases, it is not effective in all cases.

Instead, the journey to financial freedom needs divine discipline that originates from God's grace. This form of discipline empowers us to peacefully and prudently live in moderation and within our means. It inspires us to joyfully accept our current position while working and investing to make a better future.

The positive mindset of divine discipline is rooted on faith, hope, and love. It is not fixed on the negative aspects of guilt and suffering.

With divine discipline, we don't have to feel guilty to be blessed. Divine discipline focuses on God's grace instead of the situation. It is result oriented. It highlights the victory and not the task.

Divine discipline gives us the wisdom and serenity to understand and appreciate that in tough times, it's not the pain of the trial but the joy of what God is doing for us through the trial.

After all, God promises the peace and joy of prosperity not the pain and suffering of financial freedom. (Read Ecclesiastes 3:12)

Divine Discipline is a Gift of Grace

While reviving my faith, I discovered the inspiring book *Divine Discipline* (previously mentioned). The author, Dr. Rhonda H. Kelley, has captured the divine aspects of discipline that are needed to ensure God's protection.

According to Kelley, discipline is a divine gift of love and grace from God. It is essential to success in all areas of life.

"It is more than a matter of human discipline. It is a reflection of a close personal relationship with the Holy Spirit. Without self-control, we will be conformed to the world. With self-control, we will be transformed into the likeness of Christ (Romans 12:2)," Kelley stated.

One of the most important keys to accepting and utilizing God's gift of divine discipline is *effective time management*, according to Kelley.

When we become masters of our time, we keep on course and complete our plans in a timely fashion. In this way, God's grace protects us from straying from His path that leads to financial victory.

EFFECTIVE TIME MANAGEMENT CONCEPTS

"Therefore be careful how you walk, not as unwise men but as wise, making the most of your time, because the days are evil. So then do not be foolish, but understand what the will of the Lord is."(Ephesians 5:15-17 - NASB)

We cannot alter time. We can't stop it, slow it down, or stretch it. Time machines only exist in science fiction. Thus, we really can't manage time.

However, we can manage how we use it. Since everyone has 24 hours in a day, success is measured on how well we master each moment. It isn't based on the number of hours we work; it is based on how we get those hours to work for us.

As prudent (champion) stewards, we are entrusted to manage our time in a godly manner and not in a worldly way. Therefore, effective time management is critical for living a Christian financial lifestyle.

The basis for Christians to effectively master time is creating and maintaining a flexible evolving schedule. This fluid process enhances our distinctive personality while aligning our unique goals, mission, and vision with our Christian lifestyle. Hence, a winning formula for one person may not work for another.

However, four basic steps apply.

- Set all financial objectives for the next day, week, month, year, and beyond. Be less specific for objectives that are more than a week away.
- Once financial objectives are set, develop a detailed and flexible daily and weekly schedule of tasks with success times (deadlines). Divide tasks for large objectives into smaller tasks with interim success times.
- Monitor progress daily by scheduling, keeping, reviewing, and focusing on activities by writing them in a daily journal and updating your financial plan. Reflect on these updates daily.
- Remain focused. Say "no" to distractions that take time away from the vision and the mission. Don't digress or waste time on unimportant trivial things or people with negative attitudes.

Chapter 7

The Seven Building Block Strategies

WALLS DEFINE AND SECURE OUR CHRISTIAN FINANCIAL MISSION

Before implementing any strategy, contact a licensed professional.

Victory Verses

"The day for building your walls will come, the day for extending your boundaries."

Micah 7:11

*NOTE: **Although some of these strategies may not now apply to you as a teenager or young adult, they will in the future be the building blocks for your finances.***

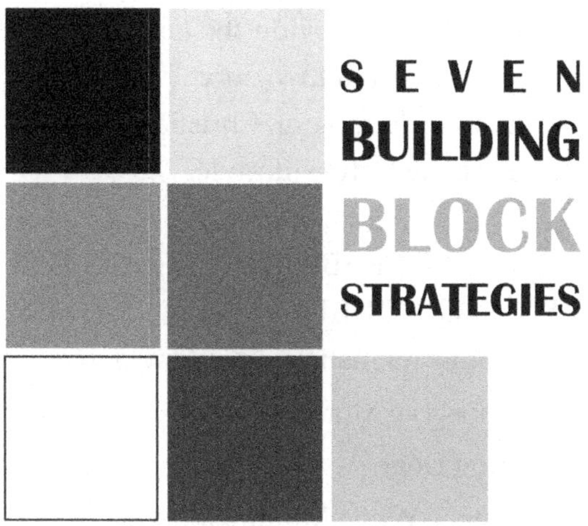

Financial Freedom Building Blocks

"Sow your seed in the morning, and at evening let your hands not be idle, for you do not know which will succeed, whether this or that, or whether both will do equally well." (Ecclesiastes 11:6)

In these uncertain times, we must, more than ever, get the most from every penny we earn. People work hard for their money. Now, we must act smarter with the way we use it.

As I was rebuilding my life, I learned that to secure God's vision of financial freedom, I needed prayer and a well-defined mission that included written goals with a plan of action. (Read Habakkuk 2:2-3 - NASB)

This action plan applied proven tactics and strategies, such as the *Seven Building Block Strategies* that create, cultivate, and conserve wealth.

These practical strategies provide the concepts that take financial goals from vision to victory. These blocks configure the walls that define our Christian financial mission. They support a debt-free lifestyle.

SEVEN BUILDING BLOCK (BB) STRATEGIES FOR TEENS AND YOUNG ADULTS

1. Develop and Follow a Financial Freedom Plan
2. Pay Less and Conserve More
3. Eliminate Existing Debt
4. Maximize Insurance While Minimizing Cost
5. Reduce Your Taxes
6. Invest in Your Future
7. Keep Your Wealth (Create Your Legacy)

The first BB strategy establishes a *Christ-centered Financial Freedom Plan* (Budget). This plan redefines and organizes monthly expenses by adhering to Christian priorities and spending guidelines.

The second BB strategy offers practical solutions to reduce expenses and create, cultivate, and conserve wealth by increasing disposable income.

The third offers tips for eliminating debt while the fourth helps cure headaches caused by insurance.

The last three strategies (5-7) work in harmony. Many of the funding accounts provide effective tactics for tax savings (5) while investing in future growth (6) that conserves and perpetuates wealth (7) for us and future generations.

Goals Shape and Define Our Future

Goals give life to our purpose by shaping the vision of our destiny and directing the path of our mission. Therefore, before implementing our proven strategies, we must first identify our Christian financial goals.

"I press on toward the goal for the prize of the upward call of God in Christ Jesus." (Philippians 3:14 - NASB)

A goal is a realistic and obtainable dream or objective of future prosperity, success, significance, or security. It must be specific, attainable, measureable, accountable, and motivational.

To stimulate achieving success, a goal should be written and have an action plan designed for obtaining the expected rewards within a specific success time (deadline).

In fact, an unverified (but often cited) Harvard study showed that students who had written goals earned ten times as much as the other students a decade later.

Unfortunately, most people don't have written goals while others confuse genuine goals with fantasies.

This mindset of wishful thinking and daydreaming is a waste of time. Instead, empower genuine goals by writing them down and then put them into action with a plan.

"Those who work their land will have abundant food, but those who chase fantasies will have their fill of poverty." (Proverbs 28:19)

BASIC CHRISTIAN FINANCIAL GOALS

- Live Financially Free (Debt-Free Lifestyle).
- Buy a Home.
- Plan for Retirement.
- Establish a College Fund for Children.
- Leave an Inheritance (Planned Gifts).

NOTE: The last three goals are discussed in BUILDING BLOCK STRATEGY 6 on page 96.

Goal Tending: Accountability

To maintain accountability to our financial goals, it is imperative to periodically monitor progress toward achieving success times (deadlines).

Be prepared for surprises that try to steer us off course. Facing challenges require flexibility, prayer, and support from mentors.

Don't be discouraged if refocusing is needed. Adapt and pray for inspiration to overcome these temporary hurdles.

All we need to do is make adjustments. This turns roadblocks into building blocks for success.

If not already done, now is the time to tend to your goals by discussing, determining, and writing them down. You may even want to rethink, clarify, or refine existing goals.

Time Frames for Goals

Realistic financial goals require realistic success times to measure progress. Thus, categorize financial goals into five specific periods. Major goals, which fall into the last three categories, often contain shorter term goals within them.

Don't set yourself up for defeat. Make sure your success times are realistic, practical, and appropriate.

- **Immediate Goals**
  Completion is required in less than 90 days.

- **Short-term Goals**
  Reward is obtainable in less than a year, but not achieved within the first three months.

- **Medium-range Goals (Major)**
  Success is expected within one to five years.

- **Long-term Goals (Major)**
  Victory is envisioned within six to ten years.

- **Lifetime Goals (Major)**
  Triumph is foreseen in more than ten years.

To learn more about the process for setting and achieving goals, see my book "Smell The Popcorn: 12 Life-changing Secrets to Pop to the Top."

BUILDING BLOCK STRATEGY 1

Develop and Follow a Financial Freedom Plan

"Know well the condition of your flocks, and pay attention to your herds; for riches are not forever...." (Proverbs 27:23-24 - NASB)

Sadly, few families, individuals, and couples are aware of their month-to-month financial position. The reason is most people don't use any form of a *Financial Freedom Plan* (budget) to manage, allocate, and monitor their monthly spending.

Instead of prudent planning, these foolish stewards blindly pay their monthly bills while hoping to have a positive balance in their checkbooks at the end of the month. This unwise behavior eventually leads to economic failure. Thus, when you make money start accounting for it with a budget.

Financial independence begins by prayerfully creating a *Christ-centered Financial Freedom Plan*. This planning starts by investing the time to redefine spending priorities based on a Christ-centered lifestyle.

It is a way of life that puts our faith and values first, instead of our ego and possessions. When God is the focus, our spending habits change. We learn to live within our financial resources and not become prisoners to debt.

In contrast, when we put luxuries as the top priority, we usually live above our means without considering the consequences. Thus, before we can get our finances right, we must get our priorities right.

The Christian financial priorities for after tax dollars are divided into seven categories.

- Christ-centered Joyful Giving
- Essentials
- Shelter
- Transportation
- Savings and Investments
- Lifestyle
- Luxuries

The primary priority for all Christians of all ages is joyful giving. Thus, it is at the top of our list. The next three are necessities with equal importance while the last three are listed by priority.

A basic itemization for five of the categories is listed on the next page. Use this list as a guide. *Giving* and *Luxuries* aren't included since they vary by individual.

DETERMINE EXPENSES BY CATAGORY

The next step is to list fixed long-term and short-term obligations along with anticipating variable monthly expenses for each item in the seven categories. To assist with the cataloguing of expenses, the *Christ-centered Financial Freedom Plan* form *(Small-scale sample on page 88)* is a valuable organizational tool. This hands-on form focuses on making Christ the center of influence for all financial decisions.

If you are having trouble determining any monthly expense, review bank statements for the past few months to establish prior payment trends.

ESSENTIALS

- Food
- Grocery Items
- Clothing
- Child Care
- Medical / Dental
- Medication
- Grooming
- Misc.

SHELTER

- Reasonable mortgage (Escrow) / Rent / HOA Fees
- Furnishing Appliances / Electronics / Computer
- Media / Wi-Fi
- Phone(s)
- Utilities
- Maintenance / Repairs
- Cleaning
- Gardening
- Security
- Misc.

TRANSPORTATION

- Reasonable monthly vehicle(s) payment(s)
- Gasoline
- Vehicle insurance
- Licenses / Fees
- Maintenance / Repairs
- Parking / Tolls
- Misc.

SAVINGS / INVESTMENTS

- Regular savings
- Emergency fund
- Investments
- Money Market
- Retirement
- College Fund
- Life insurance
- Misc.

LIFESTYLE

- Education
- Leisure / Hobbies
- Entertainment
- Clubs / Health & Fitness
- Pet Care
- Vacation
- Special day gifts
- Misc.

FOLLOW PRUDENT SPENDING GUIDELINES

Upon completing the list, calculate the total for each category. Then compare each category total to prudent spending guidelines as indicated on the next two pages. Ranges for each category will probably vary with some below the standard and some above. However, the total for all categorized expenses must not exceed 100%.

As a result of this comparison, adjustments may be needed by implementing BB strategies 2-7 and practical tactics to pay less and conserve more like those found in Chapter 8. This can be a difficult activity that often means making tough decisions. So don't forget to pray. (Read Psalm 20:4 - NLT)

The end result is a *Christ-centered Financial Freedom Plan* that empowers us to serve as champion stewards. However, the best plans for financial victory are of no value, if they are not followed.

MONITOR ACCOUNTS FREQUENTLY

To verify that our financial freedom plan is prudently followed, there are various financial software, apps, and spreadsheets to record monthly financial activities for both income and expenditures. Check with a Christian adviser to determine which record keeping option best fits your personality and lifestyle.

Frequent monitoring of all financial accounts is critical for accountability. This ongoing practice confirms we are prudently sticking to our plan.

Average Monthly Spending Percentages for each Category

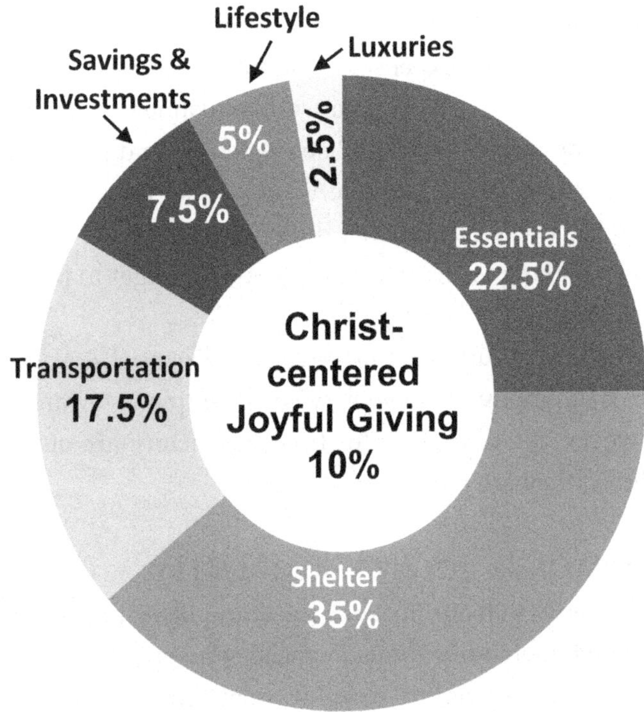

NOTE: The inner circle is larger than 10% of the entire sphere, since Christ-centered Joyful Giving has a greater impact that cannot be measured by financial parameters or worldly expectations.

Spending Percentage Guidelines

Ranges for each category of the Christ-centered Financial Freedom Plan for Champion Stewards

(Average based on $65,000 gross annual household income)

Spending Category (After Taxes)	Low %	Avg* %	High %
Joyful Giving	<10%	10%	10%>
Essentials	20%	22.5%	30%
Shelter	25%	35%	45%
Transportation	12.5%	17.5%	25%
Savings/Investments**	3%	7.5%	15%
Lifestyle	3%	5%	10%
Luxuries	0.0%	2.5%	5%

** Based on the Consumer Expenditure Survey conducted by the U.S. Bureau of Labor Statistics.*

*** Includes emergency fund, which should be a minimum of six months of your total net (after taxes) household income.*

Budgeting Apps for Beginners

Here are 12 highly effective personal budget apps (in alphabetical order) for beginners:

- **BUDGT - Daily Finance**
  Creates a daily budget and tracks your habits.
- **EMPOWER PERSONAL WEALTH**
  Tracks wealth and spending.
- **EVERYDOLLAR**
  Tracks expenses and plan finances.
- **GOODBUDGET**
  Envelope budgeting app.
- **HONEYDUE**
  Budgeting with a partner.
- **MINT**
  Tracks your income, expenses, and goals.
- **MYELOPES**
  Uses envelope system and syncs with bank accounts.
- **POCKETGUARD**
  Manages spending with ways to save money.
- **SIMPLE (PNC Virtual Wallet)**
  Combines banking and budgeting in one place.
- **SPENDING TRACKER**
  Take control of your money.
- **WALLET**
  Personal expense tracker.
- **YNAB (You Need a Budget)**
  Teaches how to budget and live within means.

BUILDING BLOCK STRATEGY 2

Pay Less and Conserve More

"So if you have not been trustworthy in handling worldly wealth, who will trust you with true riches?" (Luke 16:11)

Once we have established a *Christ-centered Financial Freedom Plan,* the next step is to handle our finances in a prudent manner. This means being money wise and strong of faith when making our buying decisions.

Chapter 8: *Debt-Free Lifestyle* features practical and easy-to-implement tactics to pay less and conserve more. This section includes over 100 ways to keep money in our pockets.

BUILDING BLOCK STRATEGY 3

Don't be addicted to avoidable debt

"Owe nothing to anyone except to love one another." (Romans 13:8 - NASB)

For the most part, being in debt is not a good thing as stated in the Bible. (Read Proverbs 22:7)

However, all debt isn't bad. In fact, *controlled debt* is a necessity in today's society. This is especially true for young adults who need to secure a place to live and transportation while many are paying tuition loans.

Thus, compare these two basic forms of debt.

CONTROLLED DEBT:

Normal monthly expenses, such as utility bills, phone bills, and insurance installments, are *controlled debt.* In practical terms, affordable home mortgages and vehicle monthly payments that fit our income along with smart credit card usage (Page 124) aren't considered *avoidable debt.* With *controlled debt,* we are the master; not a prisoner.

AVOIDABLE DEBT (Unnecessary):

The excessive amount owed to creditors for buying unessential and extravagant items is *avoidable debt,* which occurs when we live a lifestyle greater than our income. This obligation makes us prisoners to our creditors.

Eliminate unnecessary debt with these two tactics.

- **Payoff loans one at a time.**

The *Debt-free Champion Method* to eliminate debt starts by paying off credit accounts with balances under $500 by increasing monthly payments with additional funds created by implementing the *BB Strategies* and *Debt-free Lifestyle Tactics.* If there are more than one small account, start paying the one with the lowest balance first.

Once those accounts are paid, shift the money you were paying on those debts to the remaining account with the highest interest rate. Continue this process until all credit accounts are paid in full.

- **Pay more than minimum monthly balance.**

In some cases, the interest paid during the lifetime of the loan is more than the original amount borrowed.

BUILDING BLOCK STRATEGY 4

Maximize Insurance While Minimizing Cost

"This food should be held in reserve for the country, to be used during the seven years of famine that will come upon Egypt, so that the country may not be ruined by the famine." (Genesis 41:36)

Setting aside a reserve fund, as preparation for a future potential catastrophic loss, is the purpose of insurance. The key word is catastrophic. Insurance is not intended to take away all chance of risk.

Instead, it is designed to protect the policyholder from a devastating claim, such as those caused by a catastrophe. This is why many policies offer deductible or waiting period options.

As a good steward of our assets, it is important to properly protect ourselves and families along with our possessions from loss. Therefore, it is a necessity to secure protection and indemnification through insurance in order to assure our financial security in the event of an uncontrollable loss.

In addition to economic loss caused by sickness, injury, disability, or death, we need indemnification for liability suits as well as protection for property.

What is insurance?

"A fund that is established and designed for the purpose of providing protection against a substantial risk, loss, harm, or ruin.

It is defined by a (legal) contract (terms of fund disbursement and conditions) in which an insurer or underwriter indemnifies or guarantees to pay a sum of money to a policyholder (fund participant who pays a premium to the fund) in the event of a loss as stated in the contract."[2]

A well-planned insurance program, which effectively offers protection at a reasonable price, is a necessity. Prudent research and guidance from an honest and proficient agent provide competitive premiums, prevent gaps in coverage, and eliminate unnecessary and duplicate insurance. It also keeps from being over or under insured.

"Get all the advice and instruction you can, so you will be wise the rest of your life." (Proverbs 19:20 - NLT)

In order to ensure we are getting the best protection at a reasonable premium, implement the following fundamental action items.

- **Choose reputable agents and carriers.**
  It is important to check the reputation of your agent(s) and carrier(s) for stability, financial rating, professionalism, and integrity. The key is integrity.
- **Learn the basics.**
  As a prudent steward, it is critical to learn the coverages, exclusions, limitations, and conditions of policies to prevent surprises at a time of a loss. Read your policy carefully.

- **Shop for competitive premiums.**
  Before making a decision, a prudent insurance purchaser obtains at least three written quotes from more than one agent.
- **Use options wisely.**
  Delete unnecessary and excessive coverage that is costing you money.
- **Choose cost-effective deductibles.**
  When obtaining quotations, ask for several deductible options to make sure which one best fits your economic needs and risk tolerance.
- **Check the premium.**
  Confirm that your agent has checked the quoted premium for accuracy. This includes verification of classifications, discounts, and underwriting requirements. You should check too.
- **Stay claim free.**
  A small claim may cause your carrier to cancel your coverage or surcharge future policies. Be knowledgeable of how your claim affects your premium in the long run.
- **Know when not to use insurance.**
  The cost for healthcare varies drastically, even with insurance. Take for example: With my prior carrier, the co-pay for my prescription was about $8. The co-pay with my new carrier was over $42. However, by not using an insurance company, my cost was $5. Investigate what is best for you.

BUILDING BLOCK STRATEGY 5

Reduce Your Taxes

"Give to Caesar what belongs to Caesar, and give to God what belongs to God." (Matthew 22:21 - NLT)

A major portion of our hard-earned income is paid to the government through some form of tax. Federal income tax usually represents our largest tax expense.

As teens and young adults, you probably haven't been fully impacted by taxes. However, just ask your parents what they think.

Since the Internal Revenue Service has established various deductions through tax codes, we can reduce the amount of taxes we owe the Federal government through careful planning.

If legal tax strategies aren't used, we are voluntarily paying the government more taxes than required.

BUILDING BLOCK STRATEGY 5 is the process by which we increase our wealth by decreasing our tax liability through proven and legal methods.

The two spheres on the next page show the effect that tax planning has on the size of our net income. The outer edge of each circle illustrates our gross income while the inner circles represent our Christ-centered financial plan (net income). The black space between the outer edge and net income includes all taxes.

In the first sphere with no tax planning, the net income is smaller than the second with tax planning.

These graphics illustrate how tax planning increases our net income without increasing compensation.

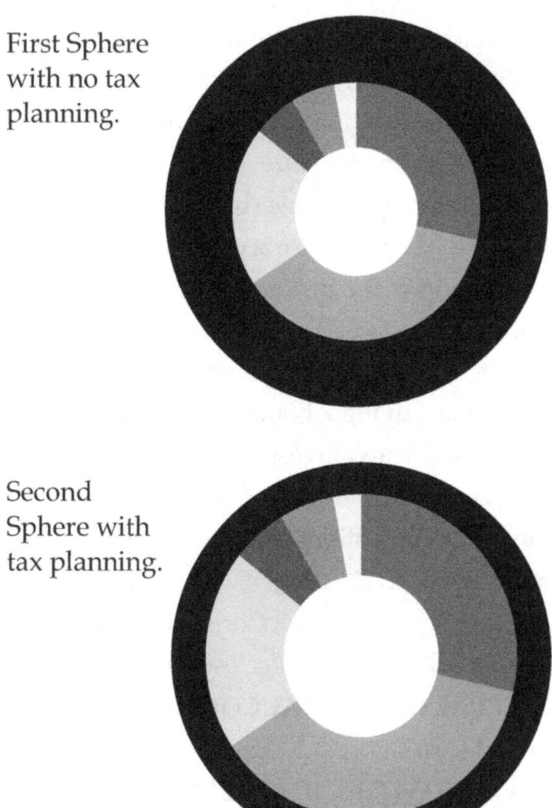

First Sphere with no tax planning.
Second Sphere with tax planning.

Effective tax reduction strategies are: Section 125 employee benefit plans (Cafeteria Plans) (Page 135); various retirement accounts (Page 97 and 138); college tuition funds (Page 97 and 144); donations to churches and charities (Page 146); and charitable trusts (Planned Gifts) (Page 101 and 147).

BUILDING BLOCK STRATEGY 6

Invest in Your Future (Put your money to work)

"Ants are creatures of little strength, yet they store up their food in the summer."(Proverbs 30:25)

When it comes to investing in our future, we need to act like the ant and wisely store (invest) part of our provisions for a later date. Proverbs 21:20 states fools spend all they earn while the wise accumulate wealth.

Prudent investing is the process of getting the most return on our assets (wealth) in proportion to our ability to tolerate risk. These investments can be as low risk and practical as buying a home. However, they can also high-risk sophisticated investment portfolios.

The best place to start our investment program is by understanding God's intentions for investing.

- **REAP WHAT YOU SOW.**
  Matthew 25:14-30 2 Corinthians 9:6
  Galatians 6:7-9 Ecclesiastes 11:1-2
- **ESTABLISH SAVINGS ACCOUNTS.**
  Proverbs 6:6-8 Proverbs 21:20
- **GIVE GIFTS WITH A JOYFUL HEART.**
  1 Timothy 6:18-19 2 Corinthians 9:8-13
- **BUILD A LEGACY (INHERITANCE).**
  Ezra 9:12 Proverbs 13:22
  Luke 15:11-24 (Parable of the Lost Son)

Wise investments enable us to achieve our future financial goals, such as retirement planning, setting up a college fund for our children, and leaving an inheritance.

Even though you are a teen or young adult, it's wise to start investing with baby steps when you start working. Be like the ant.

RETIREMENT PLANNING:

Even though retirement isn't specifically mentioned in the Bible, it's an important aspect of the planning goals for today's Christians. With the uncertainty of Social Security, prudent Christians establish individual retirement accounts.

Types of accounts: Annuity, 401(k); 403(b); and IRA. (Page 138)

COLLEGE FUND:

Children are the hope and leadership for tomorrow's world. The rising cost of education makes it a necessity to select early a savings and an investment plan designed for this need. Young adults should consider this when starting a family.

Types of accounts: 529 College Saving Plans; Prepaid tuition plans; UGMA and UTMA Accounts; and Roth IRA. Ask your parents if they have a fund for you. (Page 144)

INHERITANCE:

Our financial legacy (inheritance) is a gift of love to our family, church, charitable foundations, or cause that will benefit future generations. The book of Proverbs states that "A good man leaves an inheritance for his children's children." (Page 99)

When it comes to investing, keep the FAITH when you start working a full-time job.

F Financial Advisor

Select certified *Christian Financial Planners (CFPs)* who share your vision, faith, and values. Your advisors will assist you in creating an investment portfolio that fits your risk tolerance, funding, and goals.

A Availability

In case of an emergency, identify the withdrawal conditions (liquidity of funds), especially the early withdrawal penalty.

I Interest

Determine if the rates are guaranteed or variable. Verify that proposals and illustrations show reasonable expected future rates.

T Time

Determine the time period needed to achieve your goals. Use the power of time to compound your interest. (Example on page 141) As teens and young adults, time is on your side.

H How Much

How much can you plan to save or invest? How much risk are you willing to take with your funds?

BUILDING BLOCK STRATEGY 7

Keep Your Wealth (Create Your Legacy)

"The righteous will inherit the land and dwell in it forever." (Psalm 37:29)

I know this strategy may seem a long time from now, but you will be surprised at how quickly time passes. The older you get the faster it goes. Thus, it is never too early to learn about creating your legacy.

The way we are remembered is based on more than the wealth we accumulate during our lifetime. What matters most are the love we shared, gifts we gave, and our unselfish acts of kindness.

However, when considering our financial legacy, the way we handle our finances while we are alive directly determines what happens when we die. Since the preservation of our assets after death is as important as their accumulation, our estates must be protected from unnecessary shrinkage due to the inheritance tax.

According to the IRS, some estates that are subject to this tax shrink as much as 40%. However, the wise establishment of a *trust*[3] for legacy giving (planned gifts, page 147) can be a proactive solution to "keep our wealth" as a gift for future generations.

A *trust* can be described as a personification of a controlling entity established by a legal document for the purpose of owning, maintaining, and distributing assets and income. In technical terms, the *trust* is set up by the "grantor" who provides the assets that are placed in the *trust*, which is held and managed by the "trustee" for the welfare of another person who is called the "beneficiary."

One of the advantages of properly setting up this "fictitious legal person" is to allow the wealth of an estate to be transferred from generation to generation while avoiding the expenses and taxes incurred during the process of probate.

Probate is the legal process in which an estate is administered under the auspices of the court or other designated state entity. This administration of an estate can take several years before all accounts of the deceased are settled and assets distributed to all of the named beneficiaries and heirs.

In addition to avoiding this shrinkage that is caused by the assessments of probate, *trusts* are also created to provide lifetime income for children, elderly relatives, and/or anyone who cannot manage their assets in a reasonable manner.

However, the lack of the benefactor's ability to control the assets of the *trust,* which is common to all *trusts,* is often considered a disadvantage by the heir who is capable of handling his or her own affairs in a prudent fashion.

Two common forms used to initiate a *trust* are:

1. INTER VIVOS (LIVING TRUST) is created and operated by the grantor while they are still living.
2. TESTAMENTARY TRUST is established by the terms of a "Will" of the testator (male) or testatrix (female).

Besides determining when the trust begins, the grantor also decides if the trust is to be revocable (the grantor has the power to amend or revoke the trust) or irrevocable (the trust is permanent and final from the day it was created). This decision will determine how estate tax and gift taxes are applied.

Under an *irrevocable trust,* the process of transferring the assets of a grantor to a trustee is considered a completed transaction. Thus, if the *trust* is set up for the benefit of anyone other than the grantor, the assets are considered to be a gift to the beneficiary and are subject to the applicable gift tax.

In contrast, under a *revocable trust,* the transfer is subject to change, which means that the transaction has not been completed. Therefore, the gift tax does not apply.

TYPES OF CHARITABLE TRUST[4]

Since only outright charitable contributions and some qualified expenses are tax deductible, you should take advantage of a qualified *trust* to deduct gifts that are not a direct donation. These gifts include allowing a religious or charity organization to use and/or benefit from income generated by your property.

The common forms of qualified charitable *trusts* are the *Charitable Lead Trust* and the *Charitable Remainder Trust.*

Before setting up a trust or other form of planned gifts, contact a licensed financial advisor.

Let Your "Will" Be Done

In order to assure our wishes concerning the distribution of our estates are implemented, it is necessary to have a legal document known as a *will.* *(Not to be confused with a living will.)*[5] By definition, a *will* is testamentary, which means it is form of covenant.

A *will,* by its own conditions, expresses an intent to dispose of property and wealth at the death of the testator (male who makes the *will*) or testatrix (female who makes the *will*).[6]

Without a proper *will,* each state in the U.S. has its own laws that outline a comprehensive plan for the disposing of the estate. This plan is known as the *will of intestacy.* It has legal provisions for all possible contingencies for people who die without a valid *will.*[7]

The responsibility of regulating *wills* was given by congress to each state. Due to the variance of these regulations, it is important the *will* preparer understands state specific laws.

Also, since these laws are constantly modified and changed, *wills* can become outdated very quickly so keep up with changes and make updates. Without an update, the *will of intestacy* may be forced to apply to all or part of the estate. (Read Proverbs 13:22)

As you and your advisor start setting up a *will* or review an existing one, you may want to consider a *Durable Power of Attorney.*[8]

Debt-Free Lifestyle

Once the structure of our financial house is complete and secure, we start getting the interior (core) of our economic home in order by filling its rooms (aspects of life*) with the peace and joy of a debt-free lifestyle.

To engage, empower, and energize us with this task of feeling at home with financial freedom, Chapter 8: *Debt-Free Lifestyle* contains over 100 ways to keep money in our pockets with easy-to-implement tactics to pay less and conserve more. These tactics provide the detailed action items for the *Building Block Strategies.*

**Aspects of life – Just as the types, sizes, and number of rooms vary in each house, so do the aspects of life vary for each person. The basic categories: Emotional, Mental, Physical, Social, Spiritual, and Stewardship.*

Chapter 8

Debt-Free Lifestyle

THE INTERIOR

FILL YOUR ROOMS WITH TREASURES

TACTICS TO PAY LESS AND CONSERVE MORE

Before implementing an action plan, contact a licensed professional.

Victory Verse

"By wisdom a house is built, and through understanding it is established; through knowledge its rooms are filled with rare and beautiful treasures."

Proverbs 24:3

Debt-Free Lifestyle

Tactics to Pay Less and Conserve More

(Over 100 Ways to Keep Money in Our Pockets)

GOOD CREDIT TACTICS

INVESTMENT / TAX SAVING TACTICS

Concepts provided in Chapter 8: Debt-Free Lifestyle are some of the basic tactics that helped me stretch and conserve my money. Although successful for me, my tactics may not have the same cost-saving impact or results for you and your family.

Before implementing any tactics in the future when you have a full-time job, discuss your specific situation with licensed professionals to create financial, investment, and tax saving plans that fit your unique needs, culture, and lifestyle when you start living on your own.

Information provided in this chapter is subject to change. Even though many tactics may not apply to you now, they will be valuable tools in the future.

WISE SPENDING / SHOPPING TACTICS

Stretch Your Dollar When Shopping

It is very important for consumers to get the most for their dollar when shopping. The following action items help you obtain the greatest value for your money.

NOTE: There are many free apps to help save money on shopping, including store specific apps.[1] My examples are the apps that best fit my needs.

- **USE COUPONS / GET CASH BACK**. Instead of cutting coupons from flyers, use one are more coupon apps to get the latest coupons plus many offer cash back savings and rebates. I use **Capital One Shopping** to shop online and in stores I use **Rakuten** to get coupons, promo codes, and cash back rewards. Some other popular apps include: **Retail Me Not**; **Flipp**; **Krazy Coupon Lady**; and **ShopSavy**. Some apps are better for buying online while others are better for instore. Thus, your choice depends on where you shop, what you buy, and how you shop.
- **STOP OVERPAYING FOR PRESCRIPTIONS.** I use the free app **GoodRx** which finds the best prices to save money on prescriptions. Show the app's drug cost to the pharmacist to get discounts that are often better than most insurance prices.
- **LOOK FOR SALES**. In addition to using apps, wise bargain hunters shop several brick and

mortar (B&M) and online smaller stores who may not be connected to an app for periodic sales. They monitor the web, social media, and other media to learn when sales occur. They also sign up for emails and text-messages from stores.

- **BUY ITEMS THE NIGHT BEFORE A SALE**. If you buy your item the night before the sale originates, most stores will apply the sales price to your purchase. This way avoids the crowd and gives a better selection of sizes and colors.
- **ANTICIPATE PURCHASES IN ADVANCE**. By anticipating your needs, you are able to wait for periodic sales. This eliminates the urgency of paying full retail prices out of need.
- **USE MILITARY DISCOUNTS**. Active duty and retired military personnel and immediate family members are eligible for discounts offered by many companies. Search the web for details.
- **USE MATURE ADULT DISCOUNTS**. Several companies offer discounts for adults 55 years and older for products, services, insurance premiums, and meals. Search the web for details.
- **BUY QUALITY LESSER KNOWN PRODUCTS**. Flashy commercials and celebrity endorsements have nothing to do with quality. In fact, well-known products are often inferior to unknown brands that focus on the quality of work in lieu of ads. A wise shopper researches various product ratings and pricing before making purchases.

- **BUY SLIGHTLY DAMAGED ITEMS**. Several stores, in particular outlet stores, offer savings for slightly damaged goods.
- **PURCHASE USED ITEMS**. Before buying any new product, search various websites, such as eBay, and go to garage sales for quality used items. *NOTE: Warranties are seldom transferable.*
- **AVOID LONG-TERM CREDIT CARD DEBT.** All savings could be wasted if purchased with long-term credit instead of paying cash. You may end up paying over twice the cost of the original purchase price due to the accumulated interest.
- **COMPARE RENTING INSTEAD OF BUYING**. If you don't intend to use a product frequently, it may save you money to rent the item.
- **GET A LIBRARY CARD**. Instead of buying traditional books, audio books, movies, and music, the library has a huge selection.
- **NEGOTIATE PRICES**. Some retail outlets allow the consumer to negotiate the final price with the owner or sales manager of the store. Small stores, particularly sole-proprietors, may negotiate if they believe they may lose a sale. Don't be timid. Be firm and determined when finalizing price. If terms aren't right, walk away.
- **JOIN DISCOUNT BUYER GROUPS**. These associations, groups, or clubs allow members to purchase consumable products and other items with substantial discounts. Fees may apply.

ENERGY SAVING TACTICS

Lower Cooling and Heating Bills[1]

Heating and cooling are your two biggest energy investments, since climate control represents more than half of your monthly average bill. Not surprisingly, these are also areas where you can save a lot of money through smart energy conservation.

LOWER COOLING BILLS IN SUMMER

- In summer, I use a programmable thermostat to set my temperature at 78° when at home and 80° when out. Every degree cooler adds about five percent to my cooling bill.
- Weather stripping of outside doors and windows reduces loss of cold air in summer. (It also reduces loss of hot air in winter.)
- Consider investing in insulated windows. (Good for lowering both cooling and heating bills.)
- Install storm windows and storm doors that reduce loss of cold air in summer up to 20%. (It also reduces the loss of hot air in winter.)
- Although a slightly higher investment, consider using spray foam insulation for new construction and renovations. (Good for lowering both cooling and heating bills.)
- In summer, close your shades and draperies during the day to keep the heat out of your home.

- Caulk all cracks between door and window frames. (Good for lowering both cooling and heating bills.)
- Install awnings and overhangs to block the heat from the sun.
- Don't obstruct air vents or intake vents with shades, curtains, or furniture.
- Check air ducts for tight joints and good insulation. Cool air wasted in hot attics costs money.
- Check AC filters every 30 days to determine if they need to be cleaned or replaced. Dirty filters strain your air conditioner.
- Locate your cooling units on the shady side of your home instead of directly in sunlight. This reduces heat stress from the rays of the sun. A shade tree can help.
- Keep air circulating with a ceiling, oscillating, or box fan to place thermostat at a higher setting.
- Eliminate unnecessary interior heat by turning off unnecessary lights and appliances.
- To avoid interior humidity, conduct moisture-generating jobs like mopping, dish washing, and laundering in the cooler early morning or later nighttime hours.
- When painting your home or replacing the roof, use lighter colors to reflect heat. This lowers your cooling bill in summer but increases your heating bill in winter. The reverse is true for darker colors that absorb heat.

- Get a professional to inspect and clean cooling system in the spring.
- When purchasing a new air conditioning unit, check the energy efficiency rating. The higher the rating, the more efficient the unit. Also, buy a unit with the correct capacity for your size home.

LOWER HEATING BILLS IN WINTER

- During winter, I set my programmable thermostat at 68° when at home and 66° when out. Every extra degree of heat adds about five percent to my heating bill.
- Use sweaters and blankets instead of increasing the temperature.
- During daylight, open shades and draperies to let the solar heat of sunlight into your home. At night, close your window coverings to keep heat inside.
- Reduce heat loss by keeping attic and exterior doors closed.
- Close dampers and block flues when fireplace is not in use.
- Check furnace/heater filters every 30 days to determine if they need to be cleaned or replaced.
- Get a professional to inspect and clean heating system in the fall.
- Keep air returns or heat registers unblocked by curtains, shades, or furniture.

Lower Standby Energy Consumption[2]

Standby energy, the energy used by your electrical gadgets when not in use, can account for as much as 10% of your home energy consumption. Unplug seldom used items and place frequently used items, such as chargers, televisions, cable boxes, and small appliances, on power strips that can be switched off when not in use.

Stand-up to standby energy.

Lower Water Heating Bills[3]

After heating and cooling, maintaining hot water represents a substantial portion of your energy expense.

- Save hot water with quick showers instead of taking a tub bath.
- A water control valve in the shower head reduces hot water use that ranges from 5 to 15 gallons per minute to 2 to 3 gallons per minute.
- Fill your washer and dishwasher to capacity. A full load uses the same energy as a partial load.
- Wrap your water heater with insulation to increase efficiency by more than 10%.
- Turn the water heater off when you leave home for long periods of a week or more.

- Prevent hot water from going down the drain by fixing dripping faucets. A hot water leak that fills an ordinary cup in 10 minutes wastes more than 3,000 gallons of hot water annually.
- Set the thermostat on your water heater as low as possible as stated in the guidelines of your owner's manual.
- Close the drain on the sink basin when shaving. You pour as much as six gallons of hot water down the drain during a five-minute shave. Consider an electric razor.

Lower Kitchen Energy Consumption[4]

There are more high energy appliances in the kitchen than anywhere else in your home. Thus, managing energy use in your kitchen is one of the best recipes for saving money.

TACTICS FOR THE REFRIGERATOR

- Locate your refrigerator away from heat sources (like the range).
- Close your refrigerator doors tightly. Check and replace worn gaskets (stripping around doors).
- Limit the number of times you open the door of the refrigerator.

- Don't set your refrigerator or freezer to maximum cold. Set refrigerator temperature between 35° & 38° for the fresh food compartment; freezer at zero degrees for long-term storage.
- Turn refrigerator dial two or three settings warmer when away longer than two days.
- Use your power switch saver.
- Keep all liquids covered to prevent vapors that increase the compressor's workload.
- Clean condenser coils annually. Dirt and dust covers the coils and cause less efficient operation.
- Manual defrost refrigerators use less energy than frost-free models.
- Most side-by-side refrigerator/freezers use 45% more energy than over-under two-door models.

TACTICS FOR OTHER APPLIANCES

- Prepare several meals at one time and freeze them for later. Saves time and electric/gas cost.
- Use energy saving settings on appliances.
- Save time and energy by using microwave oven, crock pot, grill, toaster, and pressure cooker in lieu of conventional oven.
- Use pots with tight-fitting lids that hold in heat.
- Lower oven setting 25 degrees by baking in heat-retaining utensils.

Lower Gasoline Consumption

Here are simple things that you can do to reduce your monthly gasoline bill.

- **GasBuddy** is an app that searches for the best gas prices in your local area. To save more money, use the GasBuddy Card that is linked to your checking account. You can save up to 25 cents per gallon with this card.
- Checkout other free apps and websites, such as **GiantEagle.com/FuelPerks+**, that offer rewards to save you money at the pump (up to 30 free gallons) or at the grocery store (up to 20%).
- Drive sensibly. Speeding, rapid acceleration, and sudden braking can lower gas mileage up to 30% on the highway and 40% in stop-and-go traffic.[5]
- Drive slower. Every 5 mph driven over 50 mph costs additional $0.18 per gallon.[6]
- Avoid hauling cargo on roof. Roof-top cargo can reduce fuel economy up to 25% on interstate.[7]
- Keep tire pressure at proper levels.[8]
- Use the lowest grade of gasoline recommended.
- Change engine oil and air filters as recommended.
- Schedule trips in the same vicinity in one outing.
- Use carpools and public transformation.
- Limit usage of AC and heater.
- Buy fuel efficient vehicles, such as hybrids.
- Go to www.fueleconomy.gov to learn more.

FOOD COST SAVING TACTICS

Save More at the Grocery Store

The best way to become a wise gourmet is to follow these action items when grocery shopping.[1]

NOTE: There are many free apps to help save money on grocery shopping, including store specific apps. My examples are the apps that best fit my needs.

- Plan your weekly meals in order to make a list of all of your grocery needs. Instead of writing the list on paper (old school), enter the list on one of the popular free apps such as **Basket**. This app compares the total cost of your grocery list at the stores in your area to determine the store with the cheapest overall price.
- The old fashion way of cutting out coupons found in flyers is still effective but a more efficient approach is to use apps that focus on grocery shopping. These apps include **Ibotta**, **Checkout 51** and **Flipp** to name a few. All of these and similar apps basically work the same. Thus, your choice depends on where you shop and what you buy. **Ibotta** offers more rebates but can be store-specific while **Checkout 51** is easier to use and allows you to save on produce and items where coupons are scarce. **Flipp** sends coupons directly to your loyalty card at participating stores.
- If you don't want to use the above apps, you can search the web for store and manufacturer

digital coupons. These coupons can be saved in an app like **SnipSnap**. When paying, the cashier scans your phone for each coupon code.

- **Chewy**, **Petco**, and **PetSmart** are the leading apps specifically for buying pet food and supplies.
- If available, complete online grocery store survey for savings. Details usually found on receipt.
- Bring a calculator (cell phone app) with you into the supermarket. Use this to determine how discounts affect the actual cost per unit, such as cost per ounce.
- When using coupons select the smallest size of the product for the lowest cost per unit.
- Buy one or as many as you need of the # for $. Discounts are applied to each item.
- Compare the house brand products to national brands by checking the cost per unit.
- Look for advertised sales and in-store specials shown on windows and in the aisles.
- Buy generic brands and store brands.
- Buy non-perishable products in bulk during sales.
- Be patient. Wait for sales. The sales cycle usually repeats every eight to 12 weeks.
- Bake your own bread, cakes, and pastries at a savings over the packaged or store prepared.
- Have your butcher cut your selected lean meats in lieu of packaged meats.
- Substitute turkey meats, which are lower in cost and cholesterol, instead of beef.

- Buy whole chickens and cut it yourself instead of buying specific parts.
- Eliminate unhealthy snacks.
- Reduce your need for paper towels and napkins by using cloth towels.
- Total your basket of items before you check out to see if you are within your financial plan.
- Avoid temptation. Items (candy and magazines) displayed near checkout are there to tempt you.
- STICK TO YOUR LIST.
- Check your receipt for errors.
- **GET PAID TO GROCERY SHOP!** There are apps that offer cash back and rebates on items you are probably already buying. They include **Ibotta**, **Checkout 51**, **Rakuten**, and **Fetch** which turns grocery and restaurant receipts into cash.

Grow Your Own Food

It is fun and rewarding to get your hands dirty by planting seeds that grow to bear fruits and vegetables. Not only will you save on your grocery bill, but you will enjoy a diet of fresh tasting homegrown produce. By cultivating the soil you will develop pride in your green thumb. In fact, the rest of your hand will be green with the dollars you save by being a farmer.

In addition to feeding your family, extra produce could be sold at your local farmers' market.

Eat Out for Less

These are effective ways to save money when eating out.

- **USE DISCOUNT COUPONS.** Many restaurants offer discount coupons. They are available online, in apps, flyers, newspaper, or special buyers' coupon booklets. *(Base tip on the full regular price.)*
- **USE SENIOR DISCOUNTS.** Many restaurants, both large and small, family owned and fast-food chains, offer various discounts for mature adults over a certain age. Most start at 65 years of age but some offer discounts for anyone over 55. Don't be afraid to ask if you qualify.
- **DRINK WATER WITH A SLICE OF LEMON.** Instead of ordering a beverage with your meal, ask your server for a glass of water and a lemon slice that are usually free of charge. This saves up to 20% of the total cost of your meal.
- **CHOOSE COFFEE ALTERNATIVES.** Instead of buying your on-the-run coffee at an expensive chain, buy it from a gasoline/convenient store at a fraction of the cost. Look for specials.
- **COMPLETE SURVEYS.** Many chains offer rewards *(free sandwiches or drinks)* for completing a brief survey. Details are usually on the receipt.
- **LOOK FOR LUNCH OR DINNER SPECIALS.** Many restaurants offer weekday and Saturday lunch specials and early dinner specials.

Repeat, Refresh, Recycle (Renew), Replenish, and Reuse

- **REPEAT.** Instead of cooking one family meal at a time, cook in volume for multiple servings to maximize your time and food costs. The extra meals can be kept in the freezer to repeat at a later date or taken to work for lunch as a cost-saving and often healthier alternative to fast food.
- **REFRESH.** Instead of buying small bottles of bottled water, buy larger sizes and refresh your water container. The difference in cost is dramatic.
- **RECYCLE:** Champion stewards who recycle conserve energy, help the environment, reduce pollution, lower greenhouse gas emissions, and decrease waste products, such as plastics, in landfills. As stewards of God's earth, we have a moral and spiritual responsibility to keep the air, water, and land clean by recycling (renewing) waste materials into new products.
- **REPLENISH.** Some gasoline/convenient stores offer a discount when you replenish your old cup of coffee or cold drink in a recycled container.
- **REUSE.** If you make more than one pot of coffee at a time, decrease your coffee making expense without sacrificing flavor by reusing old grounds with fresh grounds. The ratio is four old portions to one fresh portion. However, for health reasons, do not reuse grounds that are over one hour old.

GOOD CREDIT TACTICS

Getting Started

Credit card companies understand that young people with no established credit need to start building credit somewhere. Since they don't want to lose out on a market of impressionable young minds there are several finance companies that offer special credit cards for this segment of the population.

However, not all are good. Choose wisely.

Here are some student-friendly credit card options:

- Capital One Quicksilver Student Cash Reward
- Capital One Platinum Secured Credit Card
- Discover It® Secured Credit Card *(No credit needed)*

Once you establish credit don't go wild with spending and don't start getting as many cards as you can. Be satisfied with one primary card.

Plastic Surgery

The average American household that carries a balance on their credit cards owes more than $16,000.[1] (Much higher in Louisiana)

According to Experian, the average American has 3.84 cards. To avoid the credit card trap, a wise consumer acts like a surgeon and cuts up all but one credit card and uses it wisely. I call this activity PLASTIC SURGERY.

However, don't cancel unused cards or reduce limits, since this hurts your credit rating. The one credit card should have a competitive interest rate, be paid in full each month, and be limited to the following practices.[2]

- **FINANCIAL GUARANTOR.** Major corporations often require a credit card to secure and guarantee payment of services and to make reservations.
- **KEEP FUNDS IN YOUR BANK ACCOUNT.** When making hotel or car rental reservations, merchants typically put a "hold" on your card for all estimated charges that include security deposits. These amounts are usually higher than your actual final expenses. Plus, if you return your car late or damaged, the rental agreement authorizes the rental company to withdraw what they determine to be an amount to cover the costs. By using a credit card, your bank account balance will not be affected.
- **FRAUD PROTECTION.** Most major credit cards, unlike debit cards, have $0 fraud liability. This means that if your credit card is used without your authority, you aren't responsible for the reported fraudulent charges.
- **EASY TRANSACTIONS.** In addition to making online shopping an efficient and safer process, credit card usage eliminates the hassle or delays in getting a credit for returns, disputes, exchanges, and price adjustments while allowing the ease of payments for tasks like filling up at the pump.

- **CASH FLOW.** Since card payments are delayed for up to 30 or more days without interest (depending on billing cycle), a credit card allows you the flexibility to purchase items when you don't have the immediate funds to pay in full.
- **EARN REWARDS AND PERKS.** Credit card issuers typically provide some sort of rewards program, such as travel miles or cash back, based on your charges. Debit cards usually don't offer rewards. Credit card perks often include free car rental insurance, product protection, extended warranties, and waived baggage fees. In some cases, perks include free flight insurance.
- **IMPROVE YOUR CREDIT SCORE.** A credit card builds your credit history if you pay the amounts due on time. Debit card usage has no impact on your credit score.
- **CREDIT REFERENCE.** Your account provides a credit reference.
- **EMERGENCY FUNDS.** Your card is available in case of an emergency.

Beware of the Teaser Rate

The most dangerous credit card trap is the zero or low percentage interest options offered for a short period.

With balance transfers of this type, an initial fee is usually charged up front. This increases your actual percentage with prepaid interest.

However, credit card companies are betting on you not paying off the balance during the special timeframe. After the period expires, the rate increases drastically. Some cards accrue interest, which is applied to your account if the balance isn't paid off during promotion.

Get Your Credit Report in Shape

Your three-digit credit score is one of the most important set of numbers in your life. Basically, your score is a snapshot of the way you handle your money. It gives creditors insight on how you pay your bills, how you've handled long-term and short-term credit in the past, and any negative findings, such as legal judgments.

A high score gets you a preferred interest rate when borrowing money, while a low score places you in either the sub-prime market or in a position that you cannot get credit on any terms.

When it comes to major purchases, such as a home or vehicle, this could mean thousands of dollars in saved interest for having an excellent credit score.

Here are seven ways to try to fix your credit.[3]

- **OBTAIN YOUR CREDIT REPORT**. You are entitled to one free credit report per year. Visit www.annualcreditreport.com to obtain your free copy. Also available from these credit reporting agencies: *Equifax, Experian,* and *TransUnion.*
- **CHECK REPORT FOR ERRORS**. In addition to checking personal information, review all of the accounts listed on your report to locate duplicate entries and items that are not for your account. Notify the credit bureau in writing of all errors.
- **DISPUTE INACCURATE NEGATIVE ITEMS**. Contact creditors who reported negative issues to the bureau so you can dispute contested items.
- **PAY SMALL DISPUTED ITEMS**. It is better to pay a creditor for a small disputed item than have your credit damaged.
- **PAY BILLS ON TIME**. Best way to establish excellent credit. This includes utility payments.
- **NEVER CANCEL CARDS/ REDUCE LIMITS.** Cancelling a card or reducing limits adversely affects your credit ratio. Your best credit score is when your debt utilization ratio is 10% to 20%.
- **RAISE YOUR SCORE WITH CREDIT APPS.** The credit app **Experian** states that it can help raise your FICO Score instantly with Experian Boost™ by including the credit for utility, cell phone, and streaming service payments you are already paying.

Buying Your First Home

One of the greatest challenges for first time homebuyers is coming up with enough money to cover the down payment and closing costs. *(See page 131 for details.)* Fortunately, there are currently several programs that can help in the form of first-time homebuyer grants that don't need to be repaid. This grant money can go towards closing costs or your down payment.

Keep in mind that the grants may have stringent qualifying requirements, such as income restrictions and the requirement to take qualifying courses.

Here are some of the current first-time homebuyer assistance programs:

- State first-time home buyer grants
- National Homebuyers Fund
- Chenoa Fund
- Fannie Mae Community Seconds
- Freddie Mac Affordable Seconds
- Good Neighbor Next Door Program
- Grants for disabled home buyers
- Grants from private lenders

In addition to these options, first-time homebuyers may qualify for local and federal tax credits, low down payment mortgages, no down payment mortgages, and more lenient approval criteria for certain types of home loans.

Check with your local real estate agent to assist you in buying your first home.

Select the Right Mortgage

When selecting a mortgage for a new home or refinancing, it is essential to consider all of the facts. Good decisions keep you from making mistakes that could last for the duration of the loan. The following are important facts to consider when securing a mortgage.

- Mortgage interest rates are affected by your credit score. Those with scores of 740+ get the best rates from lenders while those with lower scores get either higher interest rates or rejected.
- Consider if a 30 year, 20 year, 15 year, or other period is the best term for your mortgage. Keep in mind that the longer the loan period the higher the rate with more interest paid. However, the monthly payments are lower.

The following example compares 30 and 15 year mortgages. A 4.00% fixed interest rate for the 30 year mortgage and a 3.75% fixed interest rate for the 15 year mortgage are used for $100,000 borrowed. The monthly payment for the 30 year mortgage is $477.42 while the 15 year mortgage is $727.22. By paying the $249.80 a month additional payment, 180 monthly payments are eliminated. This cuts interest and total payments to the lender by almost $41,000.

- Shop for the lender with the most competitive fixed mortgage rates and closing costs.

- Closing cost includes points (prepaid interest), appraisal fees, title search, attorney fees, credit check fees, origination fees (mortgage companies processing fees), and at least one year of pre-paid homeowners and flood insurance. If you are borrowing more than 80% of your home's value, you are required to purchase private mortgage insurance (PMI), which pays lenders for losses due to the default of a mortgage.
- If you are required to obtain PMI, its first year premium is paid at closing and premiums for future years are included as part of your escrow. *NOTE: Once you have paid the mortgage balance to 80% of the original appraisal you should ask your lender to cancel the PMI. In fact, some lenders use a new appraisal to determine if you qualify to eliminate the coverage.*
- Beware of the adjustable rate mortgage (ARM). This type of loan offers a lower initial interest rate for a short period but provides lenders the option to increase the rate at a specific date in the future (usually three or five years). If you must use one, make sure it has an affordable interest cap and understand all of the conditions of the loan. However, flexible interest mortgages don't offer one of the major reasons you decided to buy a home, which is to lock in your monthly housing expense.

- Points (pre-paid interest) are included to calculate the annual percentage rate (APR). They are either added with the other closing costs to the amount due at closing or added to the amount borrowed. If you are planning to sell the home in less than seven years, it's best to secure a higher interest rate than lowering it by paying points. Why pay interest that isn't earned?
- Use the chart below to see how a change in the mortgage percentage rate affects your monthly payment. *NOTE: To determine your monthly P&I (principal and interest) payment, divide the total amount you expect to borrow by 100,000 and multiply that number by the corresponding P&I factor.*

	P&I Factor per $100,000 Mortgage		
Percentage	30 years	20 years	15 years
4.50%	506.69	632.65	764.99
4.75%	521.65	646.22	777.83
5.00%	536.82	659.96	790.79
5.25%	552.20	673.84	803.88
5.50%	567.79	687.89	817.08
5.75%	583.57	702.08	830.41
6.00%	599.55	716.43	843.86
6.25%	615.72	730.93	857.42
6.50%	632.07	745.57	871.11
6.75%	648.60	760.36	884.91
7.00%	665.30	775.30	898.83

Know When to Refinance

Refinancing existing mortgages to take advantage of lower rates can reduce the monthly payment for qualified homeowners. In fact, homeowners can decrease monthly principal and interest (P&I) payment by more than 10% because of a two percent drop in the annual percentage rate (APR). Since many factors are involved, you shouldn't make this decision hastily. Consider these questions.

How long do you plan to own your current home?

If you plan to sell your home in less than three years, your P&I reduction will probably not offset the upfront costs of refinancing.

How much of a drop in interest rate justifies refinancing?

Generally, if you plan to live in your home for more than three years, a two percent or more drop in the annual percentage rate justifies refinancing.

Would your new mortgage increase your total payout?

Don't be misled by the immediate monthly cash flow resulting from a new mortgage with a lower interest rate. If the new mortgage extends the term of your loan, the mortgage payout may increase.

Lend Money by the Book (Bible)[4]

The Bible (the book) provides Christian stewards God's wise instructions regarding lending.

Don't Co-sign or Lend Money to a Friend

As Christians, we are instructed to avoid providing loans to friends, but commanded to provide for the poor with joyful gifts and by loaning our wealth.
(Deuteronomy 15:7-8 and Proverbs 17:18)

Don't Charge Interest to God's People

God doesn't desire us to profit from lending our treasure to His deserving people, especially in their time of need. However, God commands Christian lenders to charge a proper rate to everyone else.
(Exodus 22:25 and Deuteronomy 23:20)

Limit the Term of the Loan

To avoid the huge effect of compounding interest, loans should be amortized for seven or less years. (Not practical for mortgages.) (Deuteronomy 15:1-2)

Cancel Debt of Those Unable to Pay

As a Christian lender, be prepared to release fellow Christians of their outstanding balance if they are unable to meet their obligation due to unavoidable events that were beyond their control. When you convert a loan into a gift, you receive special blessings from God. (Luke 6:34)

Hold Collateral for Loans for Some People

A prudent Christian lender needs to protect the outstanding balance with something of worldly value. On the other hand, do not accept collateral from Christians who are poor. (Deuteronomy 24:12 - NASB)

INVESTMENT / TAX SAVING TACTICS

Use a Cafeteria Plan (Section 125)[1]

A common tax reduction strategy is a Section 125 employee benefit plan (also known as a Cafeteria Plan).

This type of plan allows an employee to pay for certain qualified expenses that are not normally tax deductible with pre-taxed dollars.

This plan enables an employer to establish a written plan that allows participating employees to direct a portion of their pre-tax salary to be used to pay for approved premiums, health, dental and vision care expenses, and dependent care expenses. The taxes saved by the participating employee are federal income tax, state income tax, and FICA (Social Security and Medicare) tax.

The employee determines the current monthly or an anticipated annual cost of the selected benefits. If annual, this estimated amount is calculated as a monthly average. In either situation, the resulting figure is deducted each month from the employee's compensation before taxes. The untaxed dollars can be either contributed by the employer, the employee (in the form of salary reduction), or a combination of both.

There are three primary types of Cafeteria plans under Section 125.

- **Premium Only Plan (POP)**
- **Flexible Spending Account (FSA)**
- **Dependent Care Assistance Plan (DCAP)**

Premium Only Plans (POP)

With this basic option, employee participants pay their share of premiums for the employer's group plans (such as health, dental, and vision) with pre-tax dollars.

Flexible Spending Account (FSA)

An FSA, which are offered in conjunction with a group medical plan, allows participating employees to pay for a variety of predictable annual qualified out-of-pocket health care costs on a pre-tax basis. Items include prescriptions, routine, or special-need dental, vision care, and over the counter medication.

Dependent Care Assistance Plan (DCAP)

A DCAP (similar to an FSA) allows employees to pay approved dependent care expenses, such as qualified child day care and adult day care, with pre-tax dollars.

Cafeteria Plan Illustration	No Plan	Plan
Gross Salary	$2,500.00	$2,500.00
Less Payment of Benefit (Pre-taxed $)	NA	300.00
Taxable Salary	2,500.00	2,200.00
Federal/State Tax (20% illustration)	-500.00	-440.00
FICA (7.65%)	-191.25	-168.30
Less Payment of Benefit (Taxed $)	-300.00	NA
Net Salary	$1,508.75	$1,591.70
Net Tax Savings	NA	$82.95

Establish an HSA or HRA[2]

Due to the rising cost of health insurance premiums, more employers are offering high deductible plans that offer cost savings. As a result, an HSA (Health Savings Account) and an HRA (Healthcare Reimbursement Account) offer tax free solutions for employees to pay for deductibles and qualified expenses on a pre-taxed basis.

Health Savings Account (HSA)

An HSA works in conjunction with a high deductible HMO (Health Maintenance Organization) or PPO (Preferred Provider Organization) health insurance plan to provide a limited tax-free savings account for paying deductibles, out-of-pocket, and certain medical expenses.

An HSA account can be funded by the employee, employer, or a combination of both. It is controlled by the employee. Contributions are not subject to federal, state, FICA, or FUTA taxes up to a family and individual limit, which is established annually. (Check with your financial advisor for current conditions.)

Money can be withdrawn from the account at any time. If the money is used to cover qualified medical expenses, you never pay any taxes on it. Any money not used grows tax-deferred, like an IRA.

Healthcare Reimbursement Account (HRA)

An HRA is similar to an FSA but funded with only employer funds. With this account, the employer directs how the funds are allocated and used. All unused funds are returned to the employer at the end of the year. Employer contributions are not subject to taxes.

The Basics of Retirement Planning[3]

Even though most Christians realize that planning for retirement is important, few are willing to take the time and make the effort to implement an effective retirement plan. They prefer to procrastinate and make excuses, instead of being proactive as wise stewards. However, it is easy to understand the reasons for this apathy.

With thousands of possible investment opportunities that are governed by complex rules and regulations plus the uncertainty of interest rates and inflation, many Christians don't know how to get started. This is why prudent financial advisers are needed to help navigate through the complicated planning puzzle.

Here are some basic factors to consider:

- **STAGE IN LIFE.** As you change through the stages of life, your retirement plan needs to change too. Since the conditions (such as taxation, growth, and withdrawal penalties) vary by investment type, choose products that best fit your current stage of life. For example, when you are young, time is your ally, but excess cash may be limited due to student loans and saving for a home. Thus, strategies and products will change as you get closer to retirement age. Although your disposable income will probably be higher, time will be your enemy.

- **INFLATION.** What we pay for something today is not what we will pay for it in the future due to inflation. Just as our investments grow with time so does the cost of living. For example, if you are 36 years from retirement and the rate of inflation is 2%, your cost for an item would double when you retire.
- **LIFESTYLE.** If you desire to maintain your current standard of living, you need at least 60% to 100% of your present-day income. Although you may no longer have a mortgage payment, consider possible unexpected health related costs when anticipating future expenses at retirement.
- **LIFE EXPECTANCY.** We are living longer. Thus, the longer we live the more years of retirement we need to fund. Plus, there is a greater chance for additional health related expenses.
- **BASIC OPTIONS.** Some common investment options for retirement planning are a reverse mortgage, annuity, 401(k), 403(b), and IRAs.

Reverse Mortgage

A reverse mortgage is a type of home loan that converts a portion of your home's equity into cash. The equity can be paid as a lump sum or monthly payments to help supplement your retirement income. The funds are tax free.

Before planning to secure a reverse mortgage, investigate all of the facts and conditions, such as upfront costs, fees, and interest rates. There are many pros and cons regarding reverse mortgages.

Annuity[4]

Annuities are not for everyone. There are many pros and cons for the various types of annuities. Thus, contact your certified financial planner who has a fiduciary duty to see if an annuity is best for you now and in the future.

Basically, an annuity is a financial investment product that provides a stream of payments to an annuitant *(individual receiving payment)*. An annuity is often used by retirees, lottery winners, and lawsuit settlement recipients to turn a substantial sum of money into a steady cash flow.

An annuity consists of two phases. The *accumulation phase* is the period during which the annuity is being funded while the *annuitization phase* begins once payments start.

The way an annuity is taxed depends on how the funds are contributed. If the annuity is purchased with after tax dollars, taxes are only paid on the earned interest portion at the time of withdrawal. Conversely, if the annuity is purchased with before tax dollars, the whole amount is taxed when withdrawn.

This comparatively safe investment, which provides decent interest rates considering the low risk factor, is structured as either *fixed rate, variable rate,* or *indexed.*

- A *fixed rate* annuity offers a guaranteed rate of return for a specific period.
- A *variable rate* annuity is periodically adjusted to reflect the performance of the annuity fund's investments. Thus, there's risk.
- *Indexed* annuities offer a return based on the performance of the stock market index, but usually with a guaranteed minimum return.

Since an early withdrawal may be penalized by the government and the annuity company during the surrender period, which could last several years, an annuity isn't meant to be a short-term investment.

THE NOT SO UNIDENTICAL TWIN INVESTMENTS

Take a look at this example of how time and interest rates impact investments. David and John are identical twin brothers who did almost everything alike, except when it came to finances. Consider the following facts.

- DAVID begins annuity contributions at age 27½.
- JOHN begins annuity contributions at age 40.
- DAVID stops contributing at age 40.
  (150 monthly contributions)
- JOHN stops contributing age 65.
  (300 monthly contributions)
- The interest rate for the entire investment period for this example is 4% with an initial deposit of $100 and equal monthly contributions of $100.

Who has the largest retirement at age 65?

DAVID's retirement fund is about $800 more than JOHN's retirement fund when they are 65 years old.

Even though David started his fund earlier (150 contributions), in this scenario, it surpassed John's fund with 300 contributions. This gap increases for David when a higher rate is used. However, if the rate is 3.9% or less, John is the winner. Therefore, both time and interest rates must be considered when investing.

401(k)[5]

The 401(k) plan is the most popular investment vehicle used for profit sharing or distribution of stock bonuses. Under this plan, each employee elects to place a portion of his or her compensation into this tax deferred account.

An important feature of the 401(k) plan is the option for the employer to match a part or all of an employee's contribution. If the employer decides to participate with matching funds, the total annual contributions cannot exceed specific limitations.

403(b)[6]

The 403(b) plan is a retirement plan similar to a 401(k) plan that allows employees to contribute a portion of their salaries into individual retirement accounts. Employers eligible for this plan include public schools, churches, and other tax-exempt organizations.

IRA[7]

The Individual Retirement Account (IRA) is the tax favored personal retirement plan established by Section 408 of the Internal Revenue Code of 1974. Basically, an IRA is an investment vehicle that serves as a shell account for purchasing actual investments such as mutual funds, stocks, and bonds. You can also elect to keep your contributions in cash and earn interest on it.

All eligible employed individuals can make an annual deductible contribution with limitations. However, employees' ability to deduct their contributions may be reduced or eliminated if they or their spouses participate in an employer sponsored qualified retirement plan.

There are four basic types of an IRA.

- **ROTH IRA** - Since all contributions are made with after-tax dollars, your funds are not taxed and withdrawals are usually tax-free.

- **TRADITIONAL IRA** - Your contributions may be fully or partially tax-deductible. Earnings growth isn't taxed, but withdrawals are subject to income tax.

- **SEP IRA** - Simplified Employee Pension plan, or SEP plan, is an employer-sponsored retirement plan. Under a SEP, only employers can make contributions.

- **SIMPLE IRA** - This simple employee pension plan allows the employer and employee to make contributions.

The way contributions are made to these funds affects their taxation when they are withdrawn. Any benefits resulting from a tax deductible contribution are subject to the appropriate income tax rate.

However, any contributions made with after tax dollars are distributed with the principal being tax free while the earned interest will be taxed accordingly.

The usual 10% penalty for early withdrawal prior to age 59½ will not apply, if the funds are withdrawn due to the disability or death of the participant. The penalty is also waived if the funds are withdrawn as periodic income spread over the participants' lifetime.

Choose the Right College Fund[8]

529 College Savings Plans

Similar to IRA and 401(k) plans, 529 college savings plans are tax-free investment tools for parents to save for a child's education through a variety of options. The gains are tax-deferred. Once the funds are used to pay for qualified tuition expenses, parents do not pay taxes on the amount.

Savings in the plan belong to the parents, not the child.

Prepaid Tuition Plans

Prepaid plans, which are designed for parents who are sure that their child will attend an in-state public university, provide the same tax, financial aid, and parental protections as 529 college savings plans without the uncertainty of the stock market. This plan allows parents to pay for tuition credits in advance at a predetermined price. However, if a child goes to an out-of-state school, the full funds may not apply.

UGMA and UTMA Accounts

Uniform Gift to Minors Act (UGMA) and Uniform Transfer to Minors Act (UTMA) custodial accounts are used to hold and protect assets for minors until they reach the age of majority. The main difference between these tax-advantaged accounts is their type of assets. UGMA assets are limited to financial products, such as bank deposits, stocks, and bonds. UTMA assets can be almost any type, including real estate.

Unlike other college savings accounts, parents have no control on how the child spends the funds.

Roth IRA

To pay for education expenses, parents can establish a Roth IRA in the child's name once he or she begins earning money. Although, children over the age of 18 retain control of the accounts, early withdrawal penalties will not apply for specific spending types, such as qualified education expense.

Donate to Churches and Charities[9]

The Internal Revenue Service (IRS) allows tax deductions for certain contributions to churches and eligible charities. If you itemize, these donations can reduce your tax liability.

- **Payments made by cash, checks, credit cards, debit cards, ACH (Automated Clearing House), and online.** Keep canceled checks, receipts, or written or digital records showing the name of the charity, date, and amount of the gifts.
- **Property.** Keep written or digital records that show a detailed description and the determined value of the gifts along with the name of the charity and date of the gifts.
- **Out-of-pocket expenses for volunteer work.** Keep receipts and itemized written or digital records along with the name of the charity and date of service.
- **Use of vehicle for volunteer work.** Keep written or digital records of exact mileage and vehicle related expenses along with the name of the charity and date of service.
- **Charitable Trusts.** (Page 101)

The total of all the above contributions cannot exceed half of your Adjusted Gross Income (AGI) in any one year. Also, do not deduct any expenses that were reimbursed to you.

Create a Lasting Legacy (Planned Gifts)[10]

A planned gift is a contribution that is arranged in the present and allocated at a future date. It enables us as champion stewards to defer support to our church, schools, and charitable organizations through several gift types funded with cash, equity, or property.

Donors can choose structured gifts to be made after their lifetimes and take advantage of financial and tax benefits, which vary by country.

Individuals who reside in the United States or who benefit from U.S. tax opportunities can structure gifts that may provide financial and tax benefits, such as:

- Charitable Gift Annuities (immediate and deferred);
- Charitable Remainder Trusts;
- Pooled Income Fund; and
- Donor Advised Fund.

A planned gift creates a lasting legacy. Due to the complexity of the planning, contact a financial planner who specializes in planned gifts.

Chapter 9

Living Financially Free

THE PEACE AND JOY OF PROSPERITY

Victory Verse

"Shout for joy to the Lord, all the earth. Worship the Lord with gladness; come before Him with joyful songs."

Psalm 100:1-2

A Joyful Way of Life

"Trust in the Lord with all your heart; do not depend on your own understanding. Seek His will in all you do, and He will show you which path to take." (Proverbs 3:5-6 -NLT)

Christianity is not a sometimes thing. Christianity is a daily walk with Jesus. The same is true when it comes to living a financially free lifestyle.

At times this way of life can be challenging, but it doesn't need to be painful. Even in tough situations, when we follow God's path with divine discipline, we won't forfeit our peace and joy. With God, we rejoice. With Him, we offer praises for the opportunity to receive His blessing.

The Apostle Paul understood this concept. He found peace and joy in all occasions. (Read 1 Timothy 6:6-8) This is how Paul and Silas were able to sing praises to God while imprisoned. (Read Acts 16:25-34)

"I am not saying this because I am in need, for I have learned to be content whatever the circumstances. I know what it is to be in need, and I know what it is to have plenty. I have learned the secret of being content in every situation, whether fed or hungry, whether living in plenty or in want." (Philippians 4:11-12)

Furthermore, in Philippians 4:4-8, Paul isn't saying to rejoice for our difficulties. He's saying rejoice in the peace and joy of knowing that God is in control. Like Paul, during difficult times keep the faith. Focus on the blessings and not on the pain. Think of Paul as a role model.

"Join together in following my example, brothers and sisters, and just as you have us as a model, keep your eyes on those who live as we do." (Philippians 3:17)

I admit; this is difficult. I constantly fight the temptation that comes to steal my joy. Yet I choose not to submit to temptation. I choose to walk with God and keep my peace and joy. I choose to make godly choices.

"And the peace of God, which transcends all understanding, will guard your hearts and your minds in Christ Jesus." (Philippians 4:7)

Every day we make choices. But with God's grace, wisdom, love, and protection, we are strengthened and guided by divine discipline to make the right choices.

WARNING! Don't let sin, even the smallest sin, rob you of your financial blessings. Don't let sin affect your fellowship with God.

Don't let sin, even the smallest sin, rob you of your financial blessings.

Discipleship: Share Your Testimony of Financial Freedom

"Jesus said to the people who believed in Him, You are truly my disciples if you remain faithful to my teachings. And you will know the truth, and the truth will set you free." (John 8:31-32 - NLT)

By faithfully following God's financial truths, we experience the peace, joy, and prosperity of financial freedom. Through His truth, we are set free from the chains of debt and released from financial burdens.

Although we have come a long way, our mission and commission as financially free disciples are not finished.

Our ongoing commission is to share our peace, joy, and the truth of prosperity to all who need to be released from the bondage of debt.

"Go home to your own people and tell them how much the Lord has done for you, and how He has had mercy on you." (Mark 5:19)

As victorious stewards, we've grown into bold and confident disciples of God's financial wisdom. Thus, we are transformed from poor stewards into champion stewards whose testimonies lead by three activities.

- Role Modeling
- Teaching
- Serving

LEAD BY ROLE MODELING

"Follow my example, as I follow the example of Christ." (1 Corinthians 11:1)

Loyal disciples exemplify God's Word as revealed by Christ. Hence, integrity must be maintained in all matters.

This is especially true when it comes to handling our finances. When we lead by example, true followers of Christ lead with integrity (Page 59).

Our testimony (how we live) is the personification of our faith. (Reread Titus 2:7-8)

DWJWD™ - Do What Jesus Would Do (Page 48).

LEAD BY TEACHING

"We have different gifts, according to the grace given to each of us. If your gift is prophesying, then prophesy in accordance with your faith; if it is serving, then serve; if it is teaching, then teach." (Romans 12: 6-7)

Teaching God's master plan for financial freedom (discipleship training) keeps the momentum of our victorious testimony in perpetual motion by fortifying our commitment and conviction as champion stewards. By teaching others, we continue to learn and mature as disciples while becoming a light of hope to those in need.

"In the same way, let your light shine before others, that they may see your good deeds and praise your Father in Heaven." (Matthew 5:16)

LEAD BY SERVING THROUGH OUTREACH

"I am among you as the one who serves." (Luke 22:27)

As financially free and faithful Disciples of Christ, we must follow His example of compassion by serving through outreach evangelism. This outreach of hope enables us to witness for Christ through our loving and unselfish acts of service.

Thus, consider establishing a *Service Exchange Team* (SET) at your church as part of your outreach programs. This team provides the repair and service needs for the elderly and low-income people in the church and the entire community. A SET is a service ministry for witnessing.

"Each of you should use whatever gift you have received to serve others, as faithful stewards of God's grace in various forms." (1 Peter 4:10)

The concept is simple. Congregants with varied talents, expertise, and skills volunteer to serve those in need in a number of ways. These include home repairs, tutoring, childcare, grass cutting, house cleaning, etc. Professional services, such as basic tax preparation and insurance consulting, can also be included.

Besides encouraging a cooperative *do-it-yourself* attitude in the church, it gives members of the SET team an opportunity to witness to non-believers and to support other believers in financial need.

"Share with the Lord's people who are in need. Practice hospitality." (Romans 12:13)

Champion Stewards' 17 Essential Principles for Living Financially Secure

1. GIVE JOYFULLY *of your time, talents, treasures, love, and kindness. (Consider this your legacy.)*
2. PRAY OFTEN AND READ SCRIPTURE DAILY *for God's wisdom, direction, mercy, and blessings.*
3. GIVE THANKS AND PRAISE TO THE LORD *for your God-given gifts and blessings.*
4. PLACE CHRIST AS THE CORNERSTONE *of your finances.*
5. MAINTAIN INTEGRITY *when preparing, conducting, negotiating, and finalizing financial transactions.*
6. STICK TO YOUR CHRIST-CENTERED FINANCIAL FREEDOM PLAN *(Budget).*
7. LIVE WITHIN YOUR MEANS.
8. STOP COMPULSIVE BUYING.
9. AVOID LONG-TERM DEBT *other than reasonable vehicle and home expenses.*
10. PAY LOAN PAYMENTS ON TIME *and payoff credit card balances monthly.*
11. ESTABLISH EMERGENCY FUND *of at least six months of household net income.*
12. PLAN FOR RETIREMENT *as soon as possible.*
13. SEEK ADVICE *from Christian advisors.*
14. CHANGE, GROW, AND LEARN *from mistakes.*
15. SHOP FOR COMPETITIVE PRICES.
16. CHECK INVOICES *for errors and overcharges.*
17. SERVE WITH A SERVANT'S HEART.

Chapter 10

Finishing Touches

PURPOSE DRIVEN
FINANCIAL FREEDOM

Victory Verse

"And we know that in all things God works for the good of those who love Him, who have been called according to His purpose."

Romans 8:28

Purpose Driven Financial Freedom

"The purposes of a person's heart are deep waters, but one who has insight draws them out." (Proverbs 20:5)

God has a divine and triumphant purpose for each of us that we can either discover or never find. When we follow His victorious path, we are blessed with a life filled with peace, security, and joy. When we follow the path of the world, we are lost.

As champion stewards, who are touched by God's love (divine finishing touches), our purpose is to live debt-free to serve and honor Him. The purpose (vision) of *ChristianNOMICS*™, God's master plan for financial freedom, is driven by His love, grace, and mercy.

While the practical and spiritual wisdom, tactics, and strategies offered in this book prove valuable in creating, cultivating, and conserving wealth, they are only a starting point. Prudent *Christian Life Planning,* which keeps our financial house in order, is an ongoing process of many diversified yet coordinated decisions.

Since this process is proactive, it is essential that we (with support from professional and spiritual advice) prayerfully conduct periodic reviews of our financial position as it relates to our purpose (vision). This analysis identifies changing conditions, needs, and challenges in order to wisely respond.

"Blessed are all who fear the Lord, who walk in obedience with Him. You will eat the fruit of your labor, blessings and prosperity will be yours. (Psalm 128:1-2)

Break the Stick; Carry the Cross!

The urban term *Break the Stick* is defined as "to break up or end a relationship; break a connection."

To fully experience the joy, peace, and security of financial freedom, slothful Christians must *break the stick* of the lifestyle that created their burden of debt. They break the stick by *carrying the cross* of Christ. When free to follow God's financial plan of *ChristianNOMICS™*, His grace blesses our finances.

God's wisdom, power, and love empower us to:

Break the stick of unnecessary debt!
Break the stick of compulsive buying!
Break the stick of living above our means!
Break the stick; not the bank!
Break the stick; carry the cross!
I BROKE THE STICK!

"And whoever does not carry their cross and follow me cannot be my disciple."(Luke 14:27)

Don't Say Yes if You Don't Mean It

In Matthew we read about a father who asks his two sons to do a task. The first one says no to his father's request, but he later completes the task while the second son promptly says yes, but doesn't do it as promised.

From this parable, we learn that it is better to change your mind and do something than to make false promises. This applies to your prudent decision to live a financially free lifestyle. Make sure you mean it.

Many years ago, Hall of Fame NFL coach Don Shula told me, "It is one thing to know what to do, but it is more important to get it done."

When it comes to living a life of financial freedom, get it done. DWJWD™.

(Read Matthew 21:28-32)

The POPCORN FINANCIAL FREEDOM PLEDGE
for a Debt-Free Lifestyle

Popcorn starts with a tiny kernel that grows up to 40 times its original size when faced with extreme heat. In the same way, we can seize our opportunities to POP TO THE TOP™ of our finances by being transformed by the heat of our adversities.

Without heat, the kernel will not grow into what it's meant to be. We are like that too. Without the heat of adversity, we will not fully become the champion stewards we are meant to be.

Become a debt-free popcorn person like TOPPER (left) and POP TO THE TOP™ by taking the POPCORN FINANCIAL FREEDOM PLEDGE *(Next page)*.

(The Popcorn Person™ and Pop to the Top™ concepts are from my book, "Smell the Popcorn: 12 Life-changing Secrets to Pop to the Top.")

POPCORN FINANCIAL FREEDOM PLEDGE

I make this PLEDGE to myself, my family, and God that when I am own my own, I will not waste my time, talents, and money pursuing a lifestyle that results in the hardships of unnecessary debt.

Instead, I will faithfully follow the practical and spiritual wisdom of ChristianNOMICS™ that's built upon a prayerful foundation with Christ as my cornerstone. Upon this solid rock, I will frame my Christian financial character with the *C.H.R.I.S.T. Concepts* that apply SEVEN BUILDING BLOCK STRATEGIES and *Debt-Free Lifestyle* tactics to create, cultivate, celebrate, share, and conserve my God-given treasures.

Furthermore, I will follow the *17 Essential Principles for Living Financially Secure* that adhere to the prayerful promises, principles, and power tactics of financial victory through Christ.

Due to this lifestyle, I seek to be a financial blessing to others instead of an economic burden. With God's strength, wisdom, and grace, I face the heat of my financial challenges so I may be transformed into a champion steward.

As a champion steward, I am financially free to serve God and His people with the joyful gifts of my time, talents, and treasures.

"I have taken an oath and confirmed it, that I will follow your righteous laws." (Psalm 119:106)

Notes

Chapter 1: Getting Started

1. United States Conference of Catholic Bishops (www.usccb.org).

Chapter 2: God's Financial Wisdom

1. Burkett, Larry. *What the Bible Says About Money.* Brentwood, TN: Wolgemuth & Hyatt Publishers, Inc., 1989.
2. www.dictionary.com/browse/money
   www.businessdictionary.com/definition/money
3. Ibid.
4. U.S. National Debt Clock (www.USdebtclock.org).
5. Ibid.
6. According to Statista.com, the US national debt is projected to be 54 trillion dollars in 2034.

Chapter 5: C.H.R.I.S.T. Concepts

1. According to Maxwell Maltz, M.D., the author of *Psycho-Cybernetics,* it takes a minimum of 21 days to form a habit. However, a study published in the European Journal of Social Psychology conducted by Phillippa Lally, an ESRC Postdoctoral Research Fellow (University College London), states that it takes an average of 66 days for a new habit to form.
2. According to Dr. John MacArthur of *Grace to You,* the Old Testament tithes were a form of tax used to fund the national debt of Israel.

3. www.Chrisitanity.com – *Does God Require Me to Give a Tithe of All I Earn* by John McArthur.
4. These seven key truths of joyful giving are based on the teachings of Dr. Wayne Dyer, Dr. Charles Stanley, and Pastor Larry Stockstill.
5. www.undergroundhealthreporter.com

Chapter 7: The Seven Building Block Strategies

1. Mark H. McCormack, *What They Don't Teach You at Harvard Business School: Notes from a Street-smart Executive.*
2. (a) Gladney, Gerald. *Understanding Insurance, Stamford, CT: Longmeadow Press, 1991.*

   (b) Vaughn, Emmett J. *Fundamentals of Risk and Insurance.* New York, NY: John Wiley and Sons, Inc., 1986.
3. Kaufman, Phyllis C. and Stephen H Green. *Understanding Estate Planning and Wills.* Stamford, CT: Longmeadow Press, 1987.
4. Ibid.
5. According to alllaw.com, a *Living Will,* which is also called an advance directive, is a legal document that lets people state their wishes for end-of-life medical care, in the event they become unable to communicate their decisions.
6. Kaufman, Phyllis C. and Stephen H Green. *Understanding Estate Planning and Wills.* Stamford, CT: Longmeadow Press, 1987.
7. Ibid.

8. According to agingcare.com, a *Durable Power of Attorney* (POA) enables an elderly person, who is called the principal, to appoint an agent, such as a trusted child, family member, or friend, to handle specific health, legal, and financial responsibilities.

Chapter 8: Debt-Free Lifestyle

WISE SPENDING / SHOPPING TACTICS

1. BEWARE: Before selecting a smartphone application, consider how your digital spending habits and preferences will be tracked and stored by third party vendors.

ENERGY SAVING TACTICS

2. *Electrifying,* LA: Louisiana Power and Light, an Entergy Corporation, 1990.
3. Ibid.
4. Ibid.
5. Ibid.
6. Institute of Transportation Studies, University of California, Davis. *ECODRIVE I-80: A Large Sample Fuel Economy Feedback Field Test* (ITS-RR-13-15).
7. Estimates for the effect of speed on MPG are based on a study by Oak Ridge National Laboratory (ORNL): *Predicting Light-Duty Vehicle Fuel Economy as a Function of Highway Speed,* SAE 2013-01-1113.
8. Oak Ridge National Laboratory. 2014. *Fuel Economy and Emissions Effects of Low Tire Pressure, Open Windows, Roof Top and Hitch-Mounted Cargo, and Trailer* (SAE 2014-01-1614). Study results are based

on testing with a small sedan, a standard size SUV, a single roof-top cargo box (20" H x 40" W x 50" L), and a single rear-mount cargo tray. Cargo boxes with other dimensions or shapes may have a different effect on fuel economy.

9. Revised June 27, 2016. Estimates for fuel economy improvement from properly inflating tires assume a vehicle with an average under-inflation rate of 10% across all tires (25% for worst-case tire inflation scenarios). The rolling resistance sensitivity to tire pressure and the return factor (the ratio of the percentage improvement in fuel economy to a percentage reduction in rolling resistance) are taken from *The Pneumatic Tire* (NHTSA 2006).

FOOD COST SAVING TACTICS

1. *29 Ways to save Hundreds on Groceries* (Kerri Anne Renzulli) www.time.com/money/3481381/save-on-groceries/

GOOD CREDIT TACTICS

1. Study by ValuePenguin.
2. (a) www.nationwide.com
   (b) www.thesimpledollar.com
   (c) www.lendingtree.com
3. (a) www.transunion.com/Life/Credit
   (b) www.experian.com
4. Larry Burkett. *What the Bible Says About Money.* Brentwood, TN: Wolgemuth & Hyatt Publishers, Inc., 1989.

INVESTMENT / TAX SAVING TACTICS

1. Internal Revenue Service Rules regarding Section 125 (www.irs.org).
2. (a) Gladney, Gerald. *Understanding Insurance, Stamford, CT: Longmeadow Press, 1991.*

   (b) *Life Underwriter Training Counsel: Business Insurance Course.* Vol.4. Bethesda, MD: 1991.
3. Various Ameriprise retirement planning handouts.
4. www.investopedia.com/terms/a/annuity.asp
5. Various Ameriprise retirement planning handouts.
6. Ibid.
7. Ibid.
8. (a) www.savingforcollege.com

   (b) www.ameriprise.com/lifeevents/saveforcollege
9. Internal Revenue Service Rules regarding charitable donations (www.irs.org).
10. giving.standford.edu/planned-giving/overview/types-planned-gifts

Bibliography

Burkett, Larry. *Debt-Free Living*. Chicago, IL: Moody Press, 1989.

Burkett, Larry. *How to Manage Your Money*. Chicago, IL: Moody Press, 1975.

Burkett, Larry. *Preparing for Retirement*. Chicago, IL: Moody Press, 1992.

Burkett, Larry. *What the Bible Says About Money*. Brentwood, TN: Wolgemuth & Hyatt Publishers, Inc., 1989.

Covey, Stephen R. *The 7 Habits of Highly Effective People*. New York, NY: Simon and Schuster, 1990.

Givens, Charles J. *More Wealth Without Risk*. New York, NY: Simon and Shuster, 1991.

Gladney, Gerald. *Understanding Insurance*. Stamford, CT: Longmeadow Press, 1991.

Kaufman, Phyllis C. and Stephen H Green. *Understanding Estate Planning and Wills*. Stamford, CT: Longmeadow Press, 1987.

Kelley, Rhonda Harrington. *Divine Discipline*. Gretna, LA: Pelican Publishing Company, Inc., 1992.

LePre, C. Gerard. *God's Money-back Guarantee*. Gretna, LA: Pelican Publishing Company, Inc., 1994.

LePre, (C. Gerard) Jerry. *Smell the Popcorn*. Destrehan, LA: Joyful Life Publishing, 2018. (second edition)

Life Underwriter Training Counsel: Business Insurance Course, Vol. 4. Bethesda, MD; 1991.

Marcus, John. *Tax Bulletin Update.* Metairie, LA: 1992

Murray, Rev. Daniel A. *The Living Word in the Living Church.* Nashville, TN: Thomas Nelson Publications, 1986.

Pope, Ethan. *Financial Foundations for Living*. Hattiesburg, MS: 1992.

Sheen, Archbishop Fulton J. *Christ, The Center of Our World.* Audio tape S6.

Stewardship, Madison Heights, MI: Parish Publications, Inc., 1992.

Vaughn, Emmett J. *Fundamentals of Risk and Insurance.* New York, NY: John Wiley and Sons, Inc., 1986

Young, Arthur. *Guide to Personal Finance.* Washington, DC; Conrad and Associates, Inc., 1988

About the Author

Jerry LePre is a motivational speaker, trainer, life coach, and author who engages, energizes, and empowers business and civic organizations, churches, schools, and associations.

The diversified messages of this award-winning journalist and former co-host of WYES TV's *Pulse New Orleans* have been heard on TV and radio stations from coast to coast. He is recipient of the *Key to the City of New Orleans* for academic excellence and was twice named in *Who's Who of New Orleans* as a top executive.

Jerry's result oriented books, keynotes, coaching, and teaching inspire excellence while defining your V.A.L.U.E. CORE™.

Vision (purpose)
Attitude (perspective)
Love (passion)
Understanding (proficiency)
Energy (power)

His sessions feature bold graphics, heart-warming stories, humor, and Scripture with practical and easy-to-implement strategies.

The highly effective work of this New Orleans native isn't just about motivation; it's focused on transformation through the love, grace, and power of God.

In 2016-2017, Jerry served as an officer on the Board of Directors for the New Orleans Regional Chapter of the National Speakers Association (NSA). He is the founder of Celebrate Senior Life and a member of the *Southern Christian Writers* Guild.

Some of Jerry's other books (available on Amazon) include:

- *Go the Extra Yard – Empower the Champion within You,* Joyful Life Publishing, 2018 (Standard second edition); 2018 (Faith-based third edition);
- *Smell The Popcorn – 12 Life-changing Secrets to Pop to the Top and Beyond,* Joyful Life Publishing, 2020; and
- *The Popcorn Principle – 7 Biblical Truths to Stay at the Top,* Joyful Life Publishing, 2024;

www.JerryLePre.com
www.JoyfulLifePublishing.com

Made in United States
Orlando, FL
04 September 2024

50990950R00098